September 10, 1993

Dining In

A COLLECTION OF FINE RECIPES

SOUPS

•

SALADS & DRESSINGS

•

MEATS

•

FISH & SEAFOOD

•

PASTA

•

VEGETABLES

•

DESSERTS

CONTENTS

Soups

Nothing adds a homey, loving touch to a meal quite as much as a bowl of hearty homemade soup. There is something about it that makes us feel the cook really cares.

Soup is magical in another way, too. We now know there is some truth to the old wives' tale that soup is the ideal food for someone who is sick. That is because, in the process of simmering the stock, the vitamins and nutrients are dissolved out of the food, and become easier to digest.

Stocks for Soups and Sauces

The stock is the essence of a good soup or sauce. If the stock is weak, the final product will be weak and flat as well. Good stocks are derived from the freshest ingredients, simmered slowly.

This chapter includes recipes for beef, chicken, fish and vegetable stocks, all of which will be useful to add to your basic cooking repertory.

Basic Soup Types

Cream soups can be made with any number of ingredients, including vegetables, fish, or meat, which are thickened with starch and finished with milk or cream. Most cream soups are served puréed to a smooth consistency.

Bisque usually refers to a cream soup made with a shellfish base and generally finished with wine or sherry.

Chowder is similar to a cream soup, but the ingredients are not puréed.

Purées are usually made with legumes (such as beans, lentils or peas) as the base. The legumes also serve as the thickening agent, are often cooked in a strongly flavored stock (ham, mutton) and are sometimes finished with cream.

Bouillons are strongly flavored broths, sometimes served plain, but more often used as a base for other soups. The most common are beef, chicken, fish, tomato and vegetable.

Consommés are strong, richly flavored bouillons which have been filtered so that they are completely clear. They are sometimes served garnished with pasta, vegetables, meat, or whatever else the imagination suggests.

Cream of Tomato Rice

8 servings

½ cup	(125 mL) butter
1	small onion, minced
1	large carrot, minced
2	celery stalks, minced
4 cups	(1 L) chicken broth
3 cups	(750 mL) tomato purée
1 cup	(250 mL) chopped tomatoes
1 cup	(250 mL) flour
4 cups	(1 L) heavy cream
1 cup	(250 mL) cooked rice
¼ tsp	(1 mL) pepper
1 tsp	(5 mL) salt

In a pot, heat the butter.

Add the vegetables and sauté until tender.

In saucepan, heat the broth, tomato purée and tomatoes.

Add the flour to the sautéed vegetables. Cook for 2 minutes.

Add the cream and simmer until very thick. Slowly whip tomato broth into the cream.

Add the rice and seasonings.

Serve at once.

Cream of Tomato Rice

Beef or Chicken Stock

6-7 cups (1,5 L)

2¼ lbs	(1 kg) meaty beef bones or chicken bones
¼ cup	(60 mL) margarine (for beef stock only)
10 cups	(2,5 L) cold water
2	celery stalks, coarsely chopped
2	carrots, coarsely chopped
1	onion, coarsely chopped
½ tsp	(3 mL) salt
¼ tsp	(1 mL) pepper
pinch	rubbed thyme
pinch	dried oregano leaves
pinch	rubbed sage

In a heavy Dutch oven, brown beef bones slowly in margarine over low heat, about 30 minutes, stirring occasionally. (Chicken bones do not need to be browned.)

Add water and remaining ingredients; bring to a simmer. Simmer, uncovered, for 3 to 4 hours, skimming off any grease or scum that rises to the top.

Remove meat, bones, and vegetables. Strain through a sieve.

Chill stock and remove fat from surface.

Both stocks have best flavor after standing 24 hours. Use as required.

Fish Stock

8 cups (2 L)

5 lbs	(2,2 kg) fish, trimmings and bones
1	onion, diced
3	carrots, diced
3	celery stalks, diced
2	bay leaves
3	parsley sprigs
1	garlic clove
1 tbsp	(15 mL) salt
10	peppercorns
12 cups	(3 L) water

Cut the fish into small pieces. Place in a large pot. Add the vegetables and seasonings. Cover with water.

Heat gently without boiling. Simmer gently for 2 hours. While simmering, remove any scum which may rise to the top.

Drain through a sieve, then through a cheesecloth.

Use as required.

Vegetable Stock

6-8 cups (1,5-2 L)

¼ cup	(60 mL) butter
2	onions, diced
6	carrots, diced
4	celery stalks, diced
1	garlic clove, crushed
1 lb	(450 g) tomatoes, diced
2 tbsp	(30 mL) parsley
10	peppercorns
1 tsp	(5 mL) thyme

2	bay leaves
2 tsp	(10 mL) salt
12 cups	(3 L) water

In a pot, heat the butter.

Sauté the onions, carrots, celery and garlic until tender.

Add the tomatoes, seasonings and water.

Simmer gently until water is reduced by half.

Strain and use as required.

Court Bouillon

16 cups (4 L)

16 cups	(4 L) water
1 tbsp	(15 mL) green peppercorns
1 tbsp	(15 mL) salt
1	onion, sliced
2	carrots, chopped
1	celery stalk, chopped
1	lemon, cut in half
1 cup	(250 mL) white wine
1	bouquet garni*

Combine all the ingredients. Bring to a boil. Boil 10 minutes. Strain through a cheesecloth. Reserve the liquid.

Use liquid for cooking fish and shellfish.

* A bouquet garni is : thyme, marjoram, peppercorns, bay leaf and parsley, tied together in a cheesecloth.

Garden Pea Soup

8 servings

⅓ cup	(*80 mL*)	butter
¼ cup	(*60 mL*)	minced onions
¼ cup	(*60 mL*)	minced celery
¼ cup	(*60 mL*)	minced carrots
⅓ cup	(*80 mL*)	flour
4 cups	(*1 L*)	chicken stock
¼ lb	(*115 g*)	cooked ham, diced
2 cups	(*500 mL*)	frozen peas
2 cups	(*500 mL*)	light cream

In a pot, heat the butter.

Sauté the onions, celery and carrots until tender.

Add the flour and cook for 2 minutes.

Add chicken stock, ham and peas.

Simmer for 10 minutes.

Add the cream; simmer for an additional 10 minutes.

Serve hot.

Purée Mongole

8 servings

1 cup	(*250 mL*)	yellow split peas
2 tbsp	(*30 mL*)	butter
1		onion, minced
1		carrot, minced
2		celery stalks, minced
1		ham bone
4 cups	(*1 L*)	chicken stock
2 cups	(*500 mL*)	water
4 cups	(*1 L*)	chopped tomatoes
¼ tsp	(*1 mL*)	pepper
1 cup	(*250 mL*)	heavy cream

Soak peas overnight.

Melt the butter in a pot.

Sauté the onion, carrot and celery.

Add the ham bone, chicken stock, water and peas. Simmer until peas are tender.

Remove ham bone. Add the tomatoes and pepper.

Simmer for 10 minutes longer.

Add the cream and simmer for 2 more minutes.

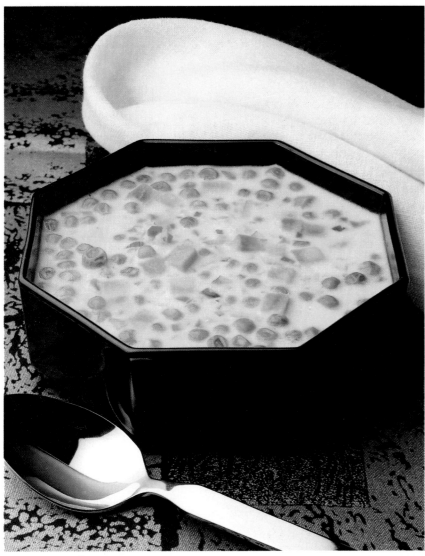

Garden Pea Soup

Vichyssoise

6 servings

4	leeks
¼ cup	(60 mL) butter
1½ cups	(375 mL) potatoes, pared and thinly sliced
4 cups	(1 L) chicken stock
1 cup	(250 mL) heavy cream
½ tsp	(3 mL) salt
¼ tsp	(1 mL) pepper
1 tbsp	(15 mL) minced chives

Trim the leeks. Discard the root and the stem ends except 2 in. (5 cm) above the white portion.

Slice and wash the leeks. Dice.

Heat the butter in an 8-cup (2 L) saucepan.

Sauté the leeks for 5 minutes. Do not brown. Add the potatoes and chicken stock.

Cover and simmer until potatoes are very tender. Press through a sieve or food mill.

Reheat and add the cream, salt and pepper. Serve garnished with chives.

Vichyssoise is usually served chilled.

Blueberry and Banana Soup

6 servings

4	bananas
3 tbsp	(45 mL) lemon juice
6 cups	(1,5 L) apple juice
¼ cup	(60 mL) sugar
1½ tbsp	(20 mL) cornstarch
½ tsp	(3 mL) cinnamon
2½ cups	(625 mL) heavy cream
2 cups	(500 mL) blueberries

In a food processor, purée bananas with lemon juice.

Place in a pot and bring to a boil with 3 ½ cups (875 mL) apple juice. Add the sugar; set aside.

Blend the cornstarch into the remaining apple juice.

Add to the soup. Simmer for 2 minutes. Remove and chill.

Add the cinnamon to the cream. Whip into soup. Stir in the blueberries.

Serve in chilled soup bowls.

Gazpacho

6 servings

2	garlic cloves, minced
2	green peppers, diced fine
3	celery stalks, diced fine
1	onion, diced fine
3 cups	(750 mL) tomatoes, peeled, seeded and chopped
3 cups	(750 mL) chicken broth
1 tbsp	(15 mL) salt
1 tsp	(5 mL) paprika
½ tsp	(3 mL) cracked black pepper
1 tbsp	(15 mL) Worcestershire sauce
1	cucumber, diced fine
3 tbsp	(45 mL) lemon juice
3 tbsp	(45 mL) olive oil
½	cucumber, sliced

In a food processor, blend the garlic, half the green peppers, half the celery, and half the onions with the tomatoes.

Pour into a large bowl. Blend in the chicken broth, seasonings, diced cucumber lemon juice and the oil.

Add the remaining green peppers, celery, and onions.

Chill 24 hours. Pour into chilled soup cups.

Garnish with sliced cucumber.

Vichyssoise; Blueberry and Banana Soup

Oyster Stew

8 servings

¼ lb	(*115 g*) bacon, diced	
3 tbsp	(*45 mL*) butter	
4	potatoes, peeled and diced	
1	onion, diced	
2	carrots, diced	
2	celery stalks, diced	
3 tbsp	(*45 mL*) flour	
4 cups	(*1 L*) fish stock	
2 cups	(*500 mL*) heavy cream	
2 cups	(*500 mL*) shucked oysters	

In a saucepan, sauté the bacon and pour off the grease.

Melt the butter and sauté the vegetables.

Add the flour and stir into a paste (roux).

Add the fish stock and cream. Stir and bring to a simmer.

Add the oysters and simmer for 30 minutes.

Old-Fashioned Chicken and Rice

8 servings

2 tbsp	(*30 mL*) butter	
1	onion, minced	
2	celery stalks, minced	
2	large carrots, minced	
3 cups	(*750 mL*) chicken, cooked and diced	
8 cups	(*2 L*) chicken broth	
1½ cups	(*375 mL*) cooked rice	
2 tbsp	(*30 mL*) chopped parsley	

In a pot, heat the butter, add the onion, celery and carrots. Sauté until tender.

Add the chicken and broth. Simmer for 15 minutes.

Add the rice and parsley. Simmer 5 more minutes.

Serve very hot.

Tomato Soup

6 servings

1 tbsp	(*15 mL*) oil	
¼ cup	(*60 mL*) minced onions	
¼ cup	(*60 mL*) minced celery	
¼ cup	(*60 mL*) minced green pepper	
4 cups	(*1 L*) chopped tomatoes	
1	bay leaf	
¼ tsp	(*1 mL*) thyme	
¼ tsp	(*1 mL*) marjoram	
¼ tsp	(*1 mL*) cracked pepper	
1 tsp	(*5 mL*) salt	
1 tsp	(*5 mL*) chopped parsley	
4 cups	(*1 L*) chicken stock	

Heat the oil in a saucepan. Add the onions, celery, green pepper and sauté until tender.

Add tomatoes, seasonings and chicken stock.

Bring to a boil; reduce and simmer 5 minutes.

Remove bay leaf and serve.

Onion Soup au Gratin

8 servings

1	French baguette stick, about 3 in. (*7 cm*) in diameter
3 tbsp	(*45 mL*) butter
2 cups	(*500 mL*) thinly sliced onions
¼ cup	(*60 mL*) all-purpose flour
5 cups	(*1,25 L*) mild beef stock
	salt and pepper
¾ cup	(*180 mL*) grated medium Cheddar
¾ cup	(*180 mL*) grated Swiss cheese
¼ cup	(*60 mL*) grated Parmesan cheese

Preheat oven to 325°F (*160°C*). Cut French bread into slices about ½ in. (*1,5 cm*) thick.

Bake in oven for 25 to 30 minutes or until bread is dry and lightly browned. Set aside.

Melt butter in a saucepan; cook onions over low heat, stirring occasionally until onions are a rich golden brown, about 30 minutes.

Sprinkle flour over onions and cook, stirring, for 2 minutes.

Add the stock, salt and pepper; simmer for about 30 minutes.

Transfer soup to serving bowls and top each with a slice of toasted bread. Combine cheeses and sprinkle over bread.

Place under heated broiler until bubbly and lightly browned.

1

Melt butter in a saucepan and cook onions over low heat until golden brown, about 30 minutes.

2

Add the beef stock, salt and pepper and simmer for about 30 minutes.

3

Transfer soup to serving bowls, top each with a slice of toasted bread and sprinkle with cheeses.

4

Place under heated broiler until bubbly and lightly browned.

Cock-a-Leekie Soup

Cream of Chicken and Mushrooms

8 servings

⅓ cup	(*80 mL*) butter
4 oz	(*115 g*) mushrooms, sliced
⅓ cup	(*80 mL*) flour
1½ cups	(*375 mL*) chicken, cooked and diced
3 cups	(*750 mL*) chicken broth
2 cups	(*500 mL*) heavy cream
¼ tsp	(*1 mL*) pepper
1 tsp	(*5 mL*) salt
2 tbsp	(*30 mL*) chopped parsley

In a pot, heat the butter. Add the mushrooms and sauté until tender.

Add the flour and cook for 2 minutes.

Add the chicken, broth, cream, seasonings and parsley.

Simmer for 15 minutes.

Serve hot.

Cock-a-Leekie Soup

8 servings

2¼ lb	(*1 kg*) stewing chicken
8 cups	(*2 L*) chicken stock
6-7	leeks, whites only
2 tbsp	(*30 mL*) butter

Gently simmer the chicken in the chicken stock for 2 ½ hours.

Add water to maintain liquid level. Remove chicken and strain liquid.

Bone chicken. Dice the meat. Cut the leeks into julienne strips.

Heat the butter in a pot. Sauté the leeks in the butter until tender.

Add the meat and broth. Reheat to a boil.

Serve very hot.

Bouillabaisse (Provençale Fish Soup)

Bouillabaisse (Provençale Fish Soup)

8 servings

⅔ cup	(160 mL) oil
1	carrot, minced
2	onions, minced
1 lb	(450 g) boneless whitefish
1 lb	(450 g) boneless pike
1 lb	(450 g) boneless ocean perch
Or 3 lbs	(1,4 kg) any firm fish

1	bay leaf
1½ cups	(375 mL) tomatoes, peeled, seeded and chopped
¼ cup	(60 mL) sherry
4 cups	(1 L) fish or chicken stock
1 doz	clams
1 doz	mussels
2 doz	shrimp, peeled and deveined
1 cup	(250 mL) lobster or crab meat
2	pimientos, diced
2 tsp	(10 mL) salt

½ tsp	(3 mL) paprika
½ tsp	(3 mL) saffron

Heat the oil in a large pot or Dutch oven. Add the carrots and onions. Sauté until tender.

Cut the fish into 1-in. (2,5 cm) strips. Add to pot and cook 5 minutes.

Add the bay leaf, tomatoes, sherry and fish stock. Cover and simmer for 20 minutes. Do not boil.

Add the shellfish, pimientos and seasonings.

Simmer for 10 more minutes.

Salmagundi

8 servings

½ cup	(*125 mL*) butter
1	carrot, diced
2	celery stalks, diced
1	onion, diced
3	large potatoes, pared and diced
⅓ cup	(*80 mL*) flour
1 cup	(*250 mL*) chopped tomatoes
8 cups	(*2 L*) fish stock
½ cup	(*125 mL*) white wine
1 tsp	(*5 mL*) salt
½ tsp	(*3 mL*) pepper
1 tsp	(*5 mL*) curry powder
1 lb	(*450 g*) whitefish, cooked and flaked

In a pot or Dutch oven, heat the butter.

Add the carrot, celery, onion and potatoes and sauté until tender.

Add flour and stir into a paste (roux). Do not brown.

Add the tomatoes, stock, wine, and seasonings.

Bring to a boil 5 minutes. Add the fish. Simmer 5 more minutes.

Pepper and Cream Cheese Soup

8-10 servings

2	large green peppers, diced
1	Spanish onion, finely chopped
3	celery stalks, thinly sliced
3 cups	(*750 mL*) sliced mushrooms
¼ cup	(*60 mL*) butter
¼ cup	(*60 mL*) all-purpose flour
6 cups	(*1,5 L*) beef stock
1	250 g pkg. cream cheese
2 cups	(*500 mL*) sliced cooked roast beef
1 cup	(*250 mL*) cooked fettuccine noodles, coarsely chopped
	salt and pepper

Sauté the vegetables in butter over medium heat until tender.

Sprinkle with flour and cook, stirring, for 2 minutes.

Gradually stir in stock and simmer until soup has thickened slightly. Stir in cheese until melted.

Add the beef slices; simmer over low heat 5 minutes, stirring constantly. Stir in the noodles.

Season to taste and serve immediately.

My Mulligatawny

8-10 servings

1	medium onion, finely chopped
2	medium carrots, coarsely grated
2	celery stalks, thinly sliced
1½ cups	(*375 mL*) sliced mushrooms
3	medium potatoes, coarsely grated
¼ cup	(*60 mL*) butter
½ cup	(*125 mL*) all-purpose flour
6 cups	(*1,5 L*) chicken stock
2 cups	(*500 mL*) milk
1	250 g pkg. cream cheese
2 tbsp	(*30 mL*) curry powder
2 cups	(*500 mL*) diced cooked chicken
	salt and pepper

Sauté the vegetables in butter over medium heat, stirring often, until tender but not browned.

Sprinkle with flour and cook, stirring, for 2 minutes. Gradually stir in stock and milk. Heat to simmering.

Stir in the cheese until melted. Add the curry powder and chicken; simmer 5 minutes.

Season to taste.

Marsala and Scallop Soup

8 servings

¼ cup	(*60 mL*) butter
1	small onion, minced
2	carrots, minced
2	celery stalks, minced
1 lb	(*450 g*) small scallops
½ cup	(*125 mL*) flour
3 cups	(*750 mL*) chicken broth
3 cups	(*750 mL*) light cream
1 cup	(*250 mL*) Marsala wine

In a pot, heat the butter. Sauté the onion, carrots and celery until tender.

Add the scallops and sauté 3 minutes.

Sprinkle with flour and cook 2 minutes.

Add the broth, cream and wine.

Simmer for 15 minutes. Serve hot.

Marsala and Scallop Soup

Nelusko (Cream of Chicken Almond Soup)

8 servings

3 tbsp	(*45 mL*) butter
½ cup	(*125 mL*) minced celery
1	small onion, minced
3 tbsp	(*45 mL*) flour
4 cups	(*1 L*) chicken stock
1 cup	(*250 mL*) light cream
¼ cup	(*60 mL*) ground almonds
1 cup	(*250 mL*) chicken meat, cooked and diced
⅓ cup	(*80 mL*) heavy cream
¼ tsp	(*1 mL*) paprika

In a 2-quart (*2 L*) saucepan, heat the butter.

Sauté the celery and onion until tender.

Add the flour and stir into a paste (roux). Do not brown.

Add the chicken stock, light cream and simmer for 15 minutes.

Add the almonds, chicken meat and heavy cream. Simmer for another 5 minutes.

Garnish with paprika.

New England Clam Chowder

10-12 servings

¼ lb	*(115 g)*	bacon, diced
½ cup	*(125 mL)*	butter
1 cup	*(250 mL)*	diced onion
1 cup	*(250 mL)*	diced celery
1 cup	*(250 mL)*	diced carrots
3 cups	*(750 mL)*	diced potatoes
1 cup	*(250 mL)*	flour
4 cups	*(1 L)*	fish stock or clam broth
3 cups	*(750 mL)*	chopped clams
3 cups	*(750 mL)*	heavy cream
¼ tsp	*(1 mL)*	pepper
½ tsp	*(3 mL)*	thyme
1 tsp	*(5 mL)*	salt

In a large pot, fry the bacon until crisp. Drain the grease.

Add the butter and vegetables. Sauté until tender.

Stir in the flour. Cook for 2 minutes. Add all remaining ingredients. Bring to a boil.

Reduce to a simmer. Simmer until thick, 15 to 20 minutes. Stir frequently.

Harry Hatch's Lobster Bisque

8 servings

¼ cup	*(60 mL)*	butter
½ cup	*(125 mL)*	minced celery
½ cup	*(125 mL)*	minced onions
¼ cup	*(60 mL)*	flour
2 cups	*(500 mL)*	fish stock
3 cups	*(750 mL)*	heavy cream
1 tsp	*(5 mL)*	salt
¼ tsp	*(1 mL)*	white pepper
¼ cup	*(60 mL)*	cream-style sherry
1 lb	*(450 g)*	lobster meat, cooked
8		lobster meat claws, cooked

Heat the butter in a saucepan. Add the celery and onions. Sauté until tender. Add the flour and stir into a paste. Do not brown.

Add the fish stock and cream. Simmer for 15 minutes. Add the salt, pepper, sherry and lobster meat. Simmer for 5 more minutes.

Press through a sieve or process in a food processor until smooth.

Garnish with the lobster claws.

Corn and Chicken Chowder

8 servings

¼ cup	*(60 mL)*	butter
1		onion, diced
4		potatoes, peeled and diced
2		carrots, diced
2		celery stalks, diced
1 cup	*(250 mL)*	corn kernels, frozen
¼ cup	*(60 mL)*	flour
4 cups	*(1 L)*	chicken stock
2 cups	*(500 mL)*	heavy cream
2 cups	*(500 mL)*	chicken, cooked and diced
1 tbsp	*(15 mL)*	parsley flakes

Melt the butter in a saucepan. Sauté the vegetables until tender.

Add the flour and stir into a paste (roux).

Add the stock and cream. Simmer 20 minutes. Add chicken and simmer 5 more minutes.

Sprinkle with parsley and serve.

NOTE : for crab or shrimp bisque change to preferred meat. Omit lobster.

Chive Cheese Soup

4 servings

¼ cup	*(60 mL)*	butter
¼ cup	*(60 mL)*	minced chives
2 tbsp	*(30 mL)*	chopped parsley
¼ cup	*(60 mL)*	flour
2 cups	*(500 mL)*	chicken broth
2 cups	*(500 mL)*	heavy cream
½ cup	*(125 mL)*	blue cheese, crumbled

In a saucepan, heat the butter, add the chives and parsley. Cook gently for 2 minutes.

Stir in the flour. Continue to cook another 2 minutes.

Add the broth and cream. Bring to a boil. Reduce to a simmer. Simmer for 10 minutes.

Crumble in the cheese. Simmer 5 more minutes.

Chive Cheese Soup

Old-Fashioned Beef Vegetable Soup

8 servings

1 lb	(450 g)	diced beef
2 tbsp	(30 mL)	barley
8 cups	(2 L)	beef stock
3 tbsp	(45 mL)	butter
1		onion, diced
2		carrots, sliced
3		celery stalks, diced
2 cups	(500 mL)	tomatoes, seeded and chopped
1 tsp	(5 mL)	salt
1/2 tsp	(3 mL)	pepper
1 tsp	(5 mL)	basil
3 tbsp	(45 mL)	soya sauce
1 tbsp	(15 mL)	Worcestershire sauce
1 tsp	(5 mL)	paprika

Gently boil the beef and barley in the stock for 30 minutes. Remove any scum that floats to the top.

In a saucepan, melt the butter and sauté the vegetables.

Add the tomatoes and seasonings.

Pour this mixture into the stock and simmer 1/2 hour longer.

Old-Fashioned Beef Vegetable Soup

Consommé

8 servings

2 cups	(500 mL)	beef stock
2 cups	(500 mL)	chicken stock
2 cups	(500 mL)	tomatoes, seeded and chopped
1		onion, diced
2		carrots, diced
3		celery stalks, diced
1		bouquet garni
1		egg white, with shell

Combine all ingredients, except egg white, and simmer. Do not boil.

Cover for one hour. Strain through muslin or cheesecloth.

Whip the egg white and whisk into soup. Add egg shell and simmer another 10 minutes.

Strain a second time through muslin or cheesecloth. Serve.

Chicken Florentine and Rice

Chicken Florentine and Rice

8 servings

1½ tbsp	(22 mL) butter
6 oz	(170 g) spinach, chopped
8 cups	(2 L) chicken broth
2 cups	(500 mL) chicken meat, diced
1½ cups	(375 mL) cooked rice

Heat the butter in a pot. Sauté the spinach for 2 minutes.

Add the chicken broth and chicken meat. Simmer for 10 minutes.

Add the rice, simmer 5 more minutes.

Serve hot.

Broccoli and Cheddar Soup

6-8 servings

4 cups	*(1 L)*	diced broccoli
3 tbsp	*(45 mL)*	butter
¼ cup	*(60 mL)*	all-purpose flour
5 cups	*(1,25 L)*	chicken stock
1 cup	*(250 mL)*	milk
1 cup	*(250 mL)*	whipping cream
1 cup	*(250 mL)*	grated medium Cheddar cheese
		salt and pepper

Sauté the broccoli in butter over medium heat until tender.

Sprinkle with flour and cook, stirring, for 2 minutes. Gradually stir in stock and milk; heat just to simmering.

Stir in cream and cheese. Allow cheese to melt in soup; season to taste and serve sprinkled with croutons.

FOR BROCCOLI AND MUSHROOM SOUP : Add 3 cups *(750 mL)* sliced mushrooms and replace Cheddar with grated Parmesan.

Egg Drop Soup

8 servings

6 cups	*(1,5 L)*	chicken stock
2		eggs
2 tbsp	*(30 mL)*	water
⅓ cup	*(80 mL)*	frozen peas

Bring chicken stock to a boil. Whip the eggs in the water.

Add the peas to the soup. Pour in the eggs in a fine stream. Cook for 2 minutes.

Serve.

Cream of Carrot and Pumpkin

10-12 servings

⅓ cup	*(80 mL)*	butter
2 cups	*(500 mL)*	grated carrots
⅓ cup	*(80 mL)*	flour
4 cups	*(1 L)*	chicken stock
1 tbsp	*(15 mL)*	lemon juice
2 cups	*(500 mL)*	pumpkin purée
¼ tsp	*(1 mL)*	ginger
¼ tsp	*(1 mL)*	nutmeg
3 cups	*(750 mL)*	heavy cream

In a pot, heat the butter.

Sauté the carrots until tender.

Add the flour and cook for 2 minutes.

Add the stock, lemon juice, pumpkin purée, and seasonings.

Simmer for 10 minutes. Add the cream; simmer for an additional 15 minutes.

Serve at once.

Cranberry and Raspberry Soup

8 servings

4 cups	(1 L)	cranberries
4 cups	(1 L)	apple juice
2 cups	(500 mL)	raspberries
¼ cup	(60 mL)	sugar
2 tbsp	(30 mL)	lemon juice
½ tsp	(3 mL)	cinnamon
2 cups	(500 mL)	light cream
2 tbsp	(30 mL)	cornstarch

Wash the cranberries. Heat the cranberries in the apple juice; simmer for 10 minutes. Press through a sieve.

Press the raspberries through the same sieve. Discard what remains in the sieve and return to a boil.

Blend in the sugar, lemon juice and cinnamon. Add 1½ cups (375 mL) cream. Mix the cornstarch with the remaining cream.

Add to soup; simmer for 5 minutes. Serve hot or cold.

Cranberry and Raspberry Soup

Blackberry Soup

6 servings

4 cups	(1 L)	blackberries
4		apples, pared, cored and diced
4 cups	(1 L)	apple juice
3 tbsp	(45 mL)	sugar
¼ tsp	(1 mL)	cinnamon
1 tbsp	(15 mL)	cornstarch
3 tbsp	(45 mL)	water

Pick over the berries — discard stems, and bruised berries.

Place berries and apples in a pot. Pour in the apple juice. Simmer for 20 minutes.

Mash with a potato masher. Strain through a sieve.

Add the sugar and cinnamon. Mix the cornstarch in the water. Add to soup. Bring to a boil. Remove and serve hot or chilled.

If served cold, you may wish to serve whipping cream with the soup.

Salads and Dressings

Salads are a great opportunity to express your creativity. You can seek out the freshest greens and vegetables, including some of the more exotic varieties becoming available in most markets, and combine them in a variety of ways so that every salad you make is a new taste experience. You can experiment with fresh herbs and even some of the increasingly popular edible flowers.

Whatever ingredients you choose, though, there are some simple rules you should follow. Choose salad greens and vegetables that are as young and as fresh as possible. Pay attention to color, form and texture, as well as flavor.

As soon as you bring your salad greens home, wash them and store them loosely wrapped in the salad crisper of your refrigerator. Assemble salads at the last possible moment, using cold ingredients and add dressing only when ready to serve. Only add enough dressing to make the salad moist.

The basic dressings for salads are mayonnaise and vinaigrette — most others are a variation of one of these. The oil should be light and flavorful, and combined with your choice of lemon juice, raspberry vinegar, or flavored vinegar. Herbs and spices should be fresh, and chosen so that their flavors enhance the final product.

Serve salads on well-chilled plates. Simply place them in the freezer 30 minutes before serving time.

Salads can fall into four basic categories:

Appetizer salads should be light and just big enough to whet the appetite. Select ingredients that will set the stage for the remaining courses.

Salad accompaniments are served with the main entrée. They should not be so sweet or tart that they overwhelm the flavors of the main dish. They can also be served after the main course, European-style, to clear the palate for the next course.

Main course salads should be hearty and flavorful. These salads should contain more than just salad greens, with enough variety to satisfy appetites as well as nutritional requirements.

Dessert salads are designed to end the meal on a sweet note, and usually involve fruit or molded gelatine.

Salade Niçoise

Salade Niçoise

4 servings

¾ cup	(*180 mL*) oil
¼ cup	(*60 mL*) vinegar
1 tsp	(*5 mL*) salt
½ tsp	(*3 mL*) pepper
½ tsp	(*3 mL*) dry mustard
2 tbsp	(*30 mL*) lemon juice
8	potatoes, peeled, cooked and diced
1	small onion, finely diced
½ lb	(*225 g*) green beans, blanched
4	lettuce leaves
4	tomatoes, peeled and quartered
4	hard-boiled eggs, quartered
10	black olives, pitted
8	anchovy filets
1 tbsp	(*15 mL*) chopped basil

Combine the oil, vinegar, salt, pepper, mustard and lemon juice.

Pour ¼ of the dressing over potatoes. Chill for 1 hour.

Toss the onion with the green beans.

Pour ¼ of the dressing over the beans and chill for 1 hour.

Toss the beans with the potatoes.

Place the lettuce leaves on plates. Top with equal portions of salad.

Arrange the tomatoes, eggs, olives and anchovies on the salad.

Drizzle more dressing over these. Sprinkle with basil and serve.

Hot Chicken & Tomato Salad

4 servings

¼ cup	(*60 mL*) lemon juice
½ cup	(*125 mL*) oil
2 tbsp	(*30 mL*) chopped parsley
1 tsp	(*5 mL*) salt
¼ tsp	(*1 mL*) thyme
¼ tsp	(*1 mL*) oregano
¼ tsp	(*1 mL*) pepper
3 tbsp	(*45 mL*) olive oil
2	garlic cloves, minced
1 lb	(*450 g*) boneless chicken, in strips
24	cherry tomatoes, halved
6 oz	(*170 g*) feta cheese, diced
1	head romaine lettuce, chopped

Blend the lemon juice, oil, parsley, salt, thyme, oregano and pepper together.

Heat the olive oil in a skillet. Add the garlic and sauté 2 minutes.

Add the chicken and brown. Pour in the dressing and heat for 1 minute.

Add the tomatoes and cheese. Heat 1 more minute.

Place lettuce on plate. Spoon chicken, tomatoes and cheese with dressing over the lettuce.

Serve at once.

Sweet and Sour Shredded Vegetable Salad

6 servings

2 cups	(*500 mL*) shredded cabbage
1 cup	(*250 mL*) shredded carrots
2 cups	(*500 mL*) shredded zucchini
4 cups	(*1 L*) bamboo shoots
½ cup	(*125 mL*) chopped green onions
½ cup	(*125 mL*) mayonnaise
3 tbsp	(*45 mL*) cider vinegar
1 tsp	(*5 mL*) salt
1 tsp	(*5 mL*) sugar
¼ tsp	(*1 mL*) pepper

Mix the vegetables together in a mixing or serving bowl.

Blend the mayonnaise, vinegar and seasonings together.

Pour over vegetables.

Sweet and Sour Shredded Vegetable Salad

Herb-Marinated Baby Mushrooms

6 servings

2	garlic cloves, crushed
1 tbsp	(*15 mL*) oil
⅓ cup	(*80 mL*) oil
1 tbsp	(*15 mL*) lemon juice
2 tbsp	(*30 mL*) chopped parsley
1 tbsp	(*15 mL*) oregano
1 tbsp	(*15 mL*) sweet basil
2¼ lbs	(*1 kg*) button mushrooms

Heat garlic in 1 tbsp (*15 mL*) oil. Sauté 1 minute.

Add remaining ingredients and pour over mushrooms.

Refrigerate 6 hours or overnight.

Curried Seafood Salad

6 servings

1 cup	(250 mL)	mayonnaise
2 tbsp	(30 mL)	lemon juice
2 tsp	(10 mL)	curry powder
½ tsp	(3 mL)	salt
½ cup	(125 mL)	minced celery
½ cup	(125 mL)	tomatoes, seeded and chopped
½ cup	(125 mL)	green pepper, minced
4 cups	(1 L)	vermicelli, broken, cooked
1 cup	(250 mL)	salmon, cooked and flaked
1 cup	(250 mL)	scallops (very small)
1 cup	(250 mL)	baby shrimp

Blend the mayonnaise, lemon juice and seasonings together.

Mix together the celery, tomatoes, green pepper and vermicelli. Combine with the dressing.

Place on a platter. Layer with salmon, scallops and shrimp.

Smoked Cheese Potato Salad

6 servings

2 cups	(500 mL)	smoked cheese, diced
3 cups	(750 mL)	potatoes, cooked and diced
2		celery stalks, diced fine
3		green onions, minced
2		hard-boiled eggs, grated
1 cup	(250 mL)	ham, cooked and diced
2 tbsp	(30 mL)	lemon juice
1 cup	(250 mL)	mayonnaise
½ tsp	(3 mL)	salt
¼ tsp	(1 mL)	pepper

Blend the cheese, potatoes, celery, onions, eggs and ham together.

Mix the lemon juice and mayonnaise with the seasonings.

Pour into the salad and toss.

Chill for 1 hour. Serve.

Dandelion Salad

6-8 servings

8 cups	(2 L)	dandelion leaves, washed and trimmed
1½ cups	(375 mL)	sliced mushrooms
2		tomatoes, cut in wedges
¼ cup	(60 mL)	croutons
¼ cup	(60 mL)	slivered almonds, toasted
½ cup	(125 mL)	golden Italian salad dressing
½ cup	(125 mL)	coarsely grated Havarti cheese

Combine dandelion leaves, mushrooms, tomatoes, croutons and almonds.

Toss with Italian dressing and sprinkle with cheese.

Spiced Lime Fruit Salad

6 servings

1	fresh pineapple
¼ cup	(*60 mL*) fresh lime juice
¾ cup	(*180 mL*) oil
2 tsp	(*10 mL*) grated lime peel
1 tsp	(*5 mL*) salt
1 tsp	(*5 mL*) cracked pepper
2 tbsp	(*30 mL*) chopped parsley
2	oranges
1 lb	(*450 g*) fresh seedless grapes
1	cantaloupe
6	romaine lettuce leaves

Peel, core and dice the pineapple.

Blend together the lime juice, oil, lime peel and seasonings.

Mix the diced pineapple into the dressing.

Cut the oranges into sections. Halve the grapes. Use a melon baller and scoop out the cantaloupe.

Mix the remaining fruit in with the pineapple. Marinate 30 minutes.

Place romaine lettuce leaves on plates.

Divide the salad equally over the lettuce.

Peel, core and dice the pineapple.

Cut the oranges into sections.

Using a melon baller, scoop out the cantaloupe.

Place romaine lettuce leaves on plates and divide salad equally over the lettuce.

Jennifer's Pear Salad

8 servings

Dressing

1 cup	(*250 mL*)	mayonnaise
½ cup	(*125 mL*)	sour cream
¼ cup	(*60 mL*)	icing sugar

Salad

10	unpeeled pears, cored and diced
½ cup (*125 mL*)	sliced almonds, lightly toasted
1 cup (*250 mL*)	diced mild Cheddar cheese
2 cups (*500 mL*)	diced seeded tomatoes
	shredded lettuce

Combine dressing ingredients; mix well and chill.

Combine pears, almonds, cheese, and tomatoes; gently toss with dressing.

Serve in nests of shredded lettuce.

Jennifer's Pear Salad

Sweet and Sour Pasta Salad

6 servings

½ lb	(*225 g*)	multicolored rotini
3		green onions, diced
½ cup	(*125 mL*)	sliced mushrooms
1		green pepper, diced
¼ cup	(*60 mL*)	almonds, toasted
4		slices bacon, diced
2 tbsp	(*30 mL*)	minced onion
3 tbsp	(*45 mL*)	sugar
3 tbsp	(*45 mL*)	vinegar
½ cup	(*125 mL*)	water
1⅓ cups	(*330 mL*)	mayonnaise

Boil rotini al dente; run under cold water until cool. Drain thoroughly.

Mix in the green onions, mushrooms, green pepper and almonds.

Fry bacon in a skillet. Add the onion and cook until tender.

Blend in the sugar, vinegar and water. Bring to a boil and reduce liquid by half.

Whip in the mayonnaise and remove from heat. Cool.

Pour dressing over salad. Blend well. Serve.

Pasta Seafood Salad

6 servings

6	tiger shrimp, butterflied
½ lb	(*225 g*) multicolored rotini pasta
6	artichoke hearts, marinated
2 tbsp	(*30 mL*) capers
1 tsp	(*5 mL*) celery seeds
3 tbsp	(*45 mL*) pimiento
1	red pepper, finely diced
½ lb	(*225 g*) baby shrimp, cooked
7.5 oz	(*213 g*) canned salmon, drained
8 oz	(*227 mL*) canned mini-corn, drained
2 oz	(*60 g*) cashews

Preheat over to 350°F (*180°C*).

Bake tiger shrimp in oven for 10 minutes. Cool.

Boil rotini in salted water al dente.

Run under cold water until cool. Drain well.

Place in a large mixing bowl.

Add the artichoke hearts, capers, celery seeds, pimiento and red pepper; toss well.

Blend in the dressing, (see above right).

Arrange baby shrimp, salmon, mini-corn, cashews and tiger shrimp on top.

Dressing

¼ cup	(*60 mL*) raspberry coulis (see *Sauces*)
½ cup	(*125 mL*) mayonnaise
½ cup	(*125 mL*) heavy cream
2 tbsp	(*30 mL*) icing sugar
1 tsp	(*5 mL*) black pepper

Combine all ingredients thoroughly.

Use as required.

Pasta Seafood Salad

Monte Cristo Salad

6 servings

Dressing

1 cup	(250 mL)	mayonnaise
1 tsp	(5 mL)	Dijon mustard
1/2 tsp	(3 mL)	chopped, fresh tarragon or 1/4 tsp (1 mL) dried tarragon

Salad

1 cup	(250 mL)	cooked, cubed lobster meat
1 cup	(250 mL)	diced cooked potatoes
1 cup	(250 mL)	sliced mushrooms
1 cup	(250 mL)	coarsely grated Swiss cheese
4		hard-boiled eggs, coarsely chopped
		romaine lettuce
1		tomato, cut in wedges

Combine the dressing ingredients; mix well and chill.

Combine the lobster, potatoes, mushrooms, cheese and eggs.

Toss gently with the dressing and arrange neatly on leaves of romaine.

Garnish with tomato wedges.

Swedish Cucumber Sour Cream Salad

6 servings

1 tbsp	(15 mL)	sugar
1 tsp	(5 mL)	salt
1 cup	(250 mL)	sour cream
3 tbsp	(45 mL)	minced green onion
2 tbsp	(30 mL)	vinegar
6		cucumbers, peeled and thinly sliced
1		small lettuce

Blend the sugar, salt, sour cream, green onion, and vinegar together.

Combine into the cucumbers.

Chill for several hours.

Serve in a bowl ringed with lettuce leaves.

Honeyed Carrot Salad

6 servings

4 cups	(1 L)	shredded carrots
2		apples, pared and diced
1/2 cup	(125 mL)	raisins
1/2 cup	(125 mL)	pine nuts
1/4 cup	(60 mL)	lemon juice
1/4 cup	(60 mL)	honey
1/4 tsp	(1 mL)	cinnamon

In a mixing bowl, combine the carrots, apples, raisins and pine nuts.

Blend the lemon juice, honey and cinnamon together.

Pour over salad.

Serve cold.

Smoked Chicken Veronique

6 servings

3 cups	(*750 mL*) diced smoked chicken
1 cup	(*250 mL*) seedless green grapes
½ cup	(*125 mL*) cashews
⅓ cup	(*80 mL*) mayonnaise
⅓ cup	(*80 mL*) lemon-flavored yogurt
3 tbsp	(*45 mL*) honey
2 tsp	(*10 mL*) cracked black pepper
6	romaine lettuce leaves
6	grape clusters

Mix the chicken, grapes and cashews together.

Blend together the mayonnaise, yogurt, honey and pepper.

Combine the chicken mixture with the dressing.

Arrange the lettuce leaves on plates.

Divide the salad equally on leaves.

Garnish with grape clusters.

Smoked Chicken Veronique

Hearts of Palm Salad

2 servings

8 oz	(*227 mL*) hearts of palm, drained
	butter lettuce leaves
¼ cup	(*60 mL*) oil
2 tbsp	(*30 mL*) lemon juice
2 tsp	(*10 mL*) minced green onion
2 tsp	(*10 mL*) minced pimiento
1 tsp	(*5 mL*) fresh cracked pepper
1 tsp	(*5 mL*) raw sugar

Arrange the hearts of palm on the lettuce leaves.

Combine the oil, lemon juice, green onion, pimiento and pepper.

Pour over hearts.

Sprinkle with sugar. Serve.

Spinach Scallop Salad

4 servings

8	slices bacon, diced
½ lb	(*225 g*) very small scallops
¼ cup	(*60 mL*) oil
3 tbsp	(*45 mL*) red wine vinegar
2 tsp	(*10 mL*) Dijon mustard
1 tsp	(*5 mL*) anchovy paste
¼ tsp	(*1 mL*) cracked black pepper
3 oz	(*90 g*) mushrooms, sliced
10 oz	(*284 g*) spinach

Sauté the bacon. Add the scallops and cook until tender.

Add the oil, vinegar, mustard, anchovy paste and pepper. Swirl and heat.

Mix the mushrooms in the spinach. Pour sauce over spinach.

Allow leaves to wilt and serve at once.

Caesar Salad

6-8 servings

3	large cloves garlic
3	anchovy filets, drained
1 tsp	(*5 mL*) seasoned salt
¼ tsp	(*1 mL*) dry mustard
1	drop hot pepper sauce
1 tbsp	(*15 mL*) Worcestershire sauce
4 tsp	(*20 mL*) red wine
2 tbsp	(*30 mL*) lemon juice
⅓ cup	(*80 mL*) white vinegar
2	egg yolks
1 cup	(*250 mL*) vegetable oil
2	heads romaine lettuce
1 lb	(*450 g*) bacon, cooked and crumbled
1 cup	(*250 mL*) croutons
¾ cup	(*180 mL*) grated Romano cheese

In food processor with steel blade, mince garlic and anchovy filets.

With machine running, add salt, mustard, hot pepper sauce, Worcestershire sauce, red wine, lemon juice and vinegar.

Add egg yolks and process until blended. With machine running, slowly add oil.

Tear lettuce and combine with bacon and croutons. Toss with dressing. Add cheese and toss again.

Shrimp & Crab Tomato Vinaigrette

6 servings

½ lb	(*225 g*) large shrimp, cooked
½ lb	(*225 g*) crab meat, cooked
4	tomatoes, peeled, seeded and chopped
1	small onion, minced
1	garlic clove, minced
½ tsp	(*3 mL*) salt
½ tsp	(*3 mL*) pepper
½ tsp	(*3 mL*) marjoram
½ tsp	(*3 mL*) basil leaves
½ tsp	(*3 mL*) dry mustard
3 tbsp	(*45 mL*) lemon juice
¼ cup	(*60 mL*) vinegar
¾ cup	(*180 mL*) oil
6	Bibb lettuce leaves
2 tbsp	(*30 mL*) chopped parsley

Mix together the shrimp, crab, tomatoes, onion and garlic.

Blend the herbs and spices together with the lemon juice, vinegar and oil.

Pour the vinaigrette over the seafood salad. Cover and refrigerate 2 hours.

Place the lettuce leaves on chilled plates, spoon the salad over the leaves.

Sprinkle with parsley and serve.

Salmon Salad Mold

6 servings

1 tbsp	(*15 mL*) unflavored gelatine
¼ cup	(*60 mL*) cold water
¾ cup	(*180 mL*) mayonnaise
3 tbsp	(*45 mL*) lemon juice
2 tsp	(*10 mL*) salt
1 tsp	(*5 mL*) white pepper
1	small onion, minced
1	carrot, minced
1	celery stalk, minced
1¼ cups	(*310 mL*) cooked, flaked salmon
2 tbsp	(*30 mL*) butter
12	jumbo shrimp, peeled deveined and cooked

Soften the gelatine in the water 10 minutes.

Blend together with the mayonnaise, lemon juice and seasonings.

Fold in the vegetables and salmon. Turn into a buttered mold.

Chill 3½ to 4 hours. Unmold and garnish with shrimp. Serve.

Salmon Salad Mold

Five Bean Salad

8 servings

1 lb	(*450 g*) canned kidney beans
1 lb	(*450 g*) canned broad beans
½ lb	(*225 g*) white beans, soaked overnight
1 lb	(*450 g*) fresh green beans
1 lb	(*450 g*) fresh yellow beans
½ cup	(*125 mL*) sour cream
¼ cup	(*60 mL*) chopped parsley
½ cup	(*125 mL*) oil
⅓ cup	(*80 mL*) lemon juice
1 tsp	(*5 mL*) salt
pinch	pepper

Drain and rinse the canned beans. Drain the white beans.

Blanch the green and yellow beans for 5 minutes.

Mix the sour cream, parsley, oil, lemon juice, salt and pepper together.

Toss the beans with the dressing and refrigerate for 3 hours.

Warm Spinach Salad

8 servings

Salad

1 lb	(*450 g*) bacon
2	10 oz (*284 g*) bags spinach
4 ½ cups	(*1,1 L*) sliced mushrooms
¾ cup	(*180 mL*) grated Parmesan cheese
3	hard-boiled eggs, coarsely chopped

Dressing

3 tbsp	(*45 mL*) Dijon mustard
4 tsp	(*20 mL*) granulated sugar
½ cup	(*125 mL*) white wine vinegar
2 tbsp	(*30 mL*) Worcestershire sauce
1 tbsp	(*15 mL*) seasoned salt
1 cup	(*250 mL*) olive oil
6	green onions, chopped

Warm Spinach Salad

Cut bacon into ½ in. (*1 cm*) pieces and fry until crisp, reserving ¼ cup (*60 mL*) drippings.

Wash the spinach, remove stems, and tear into bite-size pieces.

Toss with bacon pieces, sliced mushrooms, cheese and eggs.

To prepare the dressing, combine reserved bacon drippings, mustard and sugar in a small saucepan. Whisking constantly, bring to a boil.

Whisk in the vinegar, Worcestershire sauce, and salt.

Very slowly, add the oil, whisking constantly. Stir in the green onions and pour hot mixture over salad.

Toss and serve immediately.

Romaine Salad with Oranges

8 servings

Dressing

1 cup	(*250 mL*) salad dressing or mayonnaise
¼ cup	(*60 mL*) orange juice concentrate
¼ cup	(*60 mL*) peach or apple juice concentrate
¼ tsp	(*1 mL*) cinnamon

Salad

1	large head romaine lettuce
8	mushrooms, sliced
2 cups	(*500 mL*) grated Swiss cheese
1 cup	(*250 mL*) seedless red grapes
1 cup	(*250 mL*) fresh orange sections
½ cup	(*125 mL*) sliced almonds, toasted

Combine dressing ingredients; mix well and chill.

Wash romaine lettuce, remove stems, and tear into bite-size pieces.

Toss with sliced mushrooms, cheese, grapes and oranges.

Sprinkle almonds on top.

Serve the dressing separately.

Mayonnaise

2 cups (500 mL)

2	egg yolks
1 tsp	(*5 mL*) dry mustard
1 tsp	(*5 mL*) salt
2 tsp	(*10 mL*) sugar
⅛ tsp	(*0,5 mL*) cayenne pepper
1½ cups	(*375 mL*) oil
3 tbsp	(*45 mL*) lemon juice
1 tbsp	(*15 mL*) water

Place egg yolks in a blender. Add the mustard and the seasonings.

With the machine running, slowly pour in the oil.

Mix the lemon juice with water.

Slowly pour the lemon juice into the sauce in a steady stream while the machine runs.

Use as required. Will keep 7 days refrigerated.

Garlic & Herb Dressing

1½ cups (375 mL)

1 cup	(*250 mL*) olive oil
2	garlic cloves, minced
1 tbsp	(*15 mL*) minced parsley
¼ tsp	(*1 mL*) basil
¼ tsp	(*1 mL*) oregano
¼ tsp	(*1 mL*) thyme
¼ tsp	(*1 mL*) salt
¼ tsp	(*1 mL*) pepper
⅓ cup	(*80 mL*) vinegar

Blend together the oil, the garlic and seasonings in a blender.

With the machine running, slowly add the vinegar.

Use as salad or vegetable marinade.

French Dressing

2 cups (500 mL)

1 tsp	(*5 mL*) salt
¼ tsp	(*1 mL*) pepper
1 tsp	(*5 mL*) sugar
1 tsp	(*5 mL*) paprika
1	garlic clove, minced
1½ cups	(*375 mL*) oil
½ cup	(*125 mL*) vinegar

Mix the seasonings and garlic into the oil. Slowly whisk in the vinegar.

Fresh Tomato Dressing

2 cups (500 mL)

1 cup	(250 mL) tomatoes, peeled, seeded and chopped
¼ cup	(60 mL) honey
1 tsp	(5 mL) Worcestershire sauce
½ tsp	(3 mL) dry mustard
1 tsp	(5 mL) salt
2 tsp	(10 mL) oregano
½ tsp	(3 mL) fresh cracked black pepper
3 tbsp	(45 mL) lemon juice
¼ cup	(60 mL) vinegar
¾ cup	(180 mL) safflower oil

Place all ingredients into a blender.

Blend for 1 minute or until a smooth sauce is formed.

Use as required.

Green Goddess Salad Dressing

2 ½ cups (625 mL)

1 oz	(30 g) anchovy paste
1	garlic clove, minced
2	green onions, chopped
1 tbsp	(15 mL) parsley flakes
1 tbsp	(15 mL) chopped tarragon
1 tbsp	(15 mL) chopped chives
2	egg yolks
2 cups	(500 mL) oil
¼ cup	(60 mL) lemon juice

In a blender, purée the anchovy paste, garlic, green onions, parsley, tarragon and chives.

Add the egg yolks. With the machine running slowly, pour in the oil. Add the lemon juice.

Use for salads, chicken or cold seafood dishes.

Italian Salad Dressing

2¼ cups (560 mL)

2 cups	(500 mL) French dressing
1 tsp	(5 mL) salt
2 tbsp	(30 mL) sugar
1 tsp	(5 mL) dry mustard
1 tsp	(5 mL) paprika
½ tsp	(3 mL) oregano
½ tsp	(3 mL) basil
½ tsp	(3 mL) chervil
2 tsp	(10 mL) Worcestershire sauce

Blend the dressing with the seasonings.

Use as required.

Russian Dressing

2 cups (500 mL)

1 cup	(250 mL) mayonnaise
⅓ cup	(80 mL) chili sauce
3 tbsp	(45 mL) minced green onion
2 tbsp	(30 mL) chopped pickled beets
1 tbsp	(15 mL) chopped parsley
2 tbsp	(30 mL) chopped pitted black olives
2 tbsp	(30 mL) caviar

Blend all ingredients thoroughly.

Refrigerate. Use as required.

Green Goddess Salad Dressing, Italian Salad Dressing and French Dressing

Creamy Basil Dressing

1 cup (250 mL)

2	shallots, minced
2 tbsp	*(30 mL)* fresh basil, minced
1 tsp	*(5 mL)* Dijon mustard
½ cup	*(125 mL)* olive oil
¼ tsp	*(1 mL)* salt
¼ tsp	*(1 mL)* pepper
3 tbsp	*(45 mL)* lemon juice

Combine the shallots, basil, mustard, oil, salt and pepper in a blender.

With the machine running slowly, pour in the lemon juice.

Use as a salad marinade or dressing.

Piquant Dressing

2 cups (500 mL)

¼ cup	*(50 mL)* minced sweet red bell pepper
3 tbsp	*(45 mL)* minced onion
1 tsp	*(15 mL)* chopped capers
2 tbsp	*(30 mL)* minced dill pickles
¼ cup	*(60 mL)* sugar
1 tsp	*(5 mL)* salt
1 tsp	*(5 mL)* dry mustard
1 tsp	*(5 mL)* garlic powder
2 tsp	*(10 mL)* basil leaves
½ tsp	*(3 mL)* cracked black pepper
½ tsp	*(3 mL)* Worcestershire sauce
3 tbsp	*(45 mL)* lemon juice
¼ cup	*(60 mL)* vinegar
¾ cup	*(180 mL)* safflower oil

Place all the ingredients, except the oil, in a blender.

Blend on medium speed for 30 seconds. With machine running, slowly add the oil. Blend until smooth.

Use as required.

Honey Lemon Dressing

1¼ cups (310 mL)

1 cup	*(250 mL)* French dressing
¼ cup	*(60 mL)* honey
2 tbsp	*(30 mL)* lemon juice
1 tsp	*(5 mL)* ground cinnamon

Blend together the dressing, honey, lemon juice and cinnamon thoroughly.

Refrigerate. Use as required.

Ranch Dressing

2 cups (500 mL)

½ cup	*(125 mL)* buttermilk
1 cup	*(250 mL)* mayonnaise
2 tbsp	*(30 mL)* minced chives
1 tbsp	*(15 mL)* lemon juice
¼ tsp	*(1 mL)* salt
pinch	white pepper

Fold the buttermilk into the mayonnaise. Whip in the remaining ingredients. Refrigerate.

Use as required.

1000 Island Dressing and Blue Cheese Dressing

1000 Island Dressing

2 cups (500 mL)

1 cup	(250 mL)	mayonnaise
½ cup	(125 mL)	chili sauce
¼ cup	(60 mL)	pickle relish
½ tsp	(3 mL)	dry mustard
½ tsp	(3 mL)	basil
1 tbsp	(15 mL)	pimiento
2		hard-boiled eggs, grated

Blend all the ingredients together thoroughly. Refrigerate.

Use as required.

Poppy Seed Dressing

2 cups (500 mL)

1½ cups	(375 mL)	French dressing
⅓ cup	(80 mL)	sugar
2 tbsp	(30 mL)	poppy seeds

Blend the ingredients together thoroughly. Refrigirate.

Use as required.

Blue Cheese Dressing

2 cups (500 mL)

¼ cup	(60 mL)	blue cheese
1½ cups	(375 mL)	mayonnaise
1 tbsp	(15 mL)	lemon juice
½ tsp	(3 mL)	salt
¼ tsp	(1 mL)	white pepper

Melt the cheese over a double boiler. Remove from heat.

Place in a mixing bowl. Fold in the mayonnaise, lemon juice and seasonings.

Refrigerate. Use as required.

If desired, crumble ½ cup (125 mL) cheese into dressing.

Beef

Most people have fond memories of their favorite meal, and it almost invariably includes beef — whether it was the Sunday roast served with potatoes and gravy, or the perfect little steak in that intimate little French restaurant.

Whichever your personal favorite, it is important to select an appropriate cut of beef from a reputable butcher, and then treat it with respect during its preparation.

Tender cuts include steaks such as T-bone, Porterhouse, club, filet, sirloin and tenderloin, as well as roasts cut from the loin, sirloin, or rib section, such as rib roast and Chateaubriand.

These cuts should be treated to a dry heat cooking method, which includes roasting, broiling, pan-broiling, barbecuing, and frying.

Less tender cuts should be treated to moist heat methods such as braising, stewing, and pot roasting. Look for cuts such as brisket, chuck, flank and neck.

Timetable for Roast Beef oven temperature 325˚F (*160˚C*)			
	Minutes per lb (*450g*)		
	Rare	Medium	Well done
Rib roast 6-8 lbs (*3-4 kg*)	16	21	26
Rolled roast 6-8 lbs (*3-4 kg*)	27	34	44
Broiled steak 1 in. (*2,5 cm*) thick	12	15	20
1½ in. (*3,5 cm*) thick	15	20	25
2 in. (*5 cm*) thick	25	30	35

Steak au Poivre

6 servings

6	10 oz (*280 g*) New York strip loin steaks
¼ cup	(*60 mL*) crushed black peppercorns
¼ cup	(*60 mL*) butter
2 tbsp	(*30 mL*) brandy
1 cup	(*250 mL*) demi-glace (see *Sauces*)
2 tbsp	(*30 mL*) sherry
¼ cup	(*60 mL*) heavy cream

Pat the peppercorns into the steaks.

Heat the butter and sauté the steaks to desired doneness. Remove and keep hot.

Pour in brandy and flambé; add sherry and demi-glace.

Simmer for 1 minute. Add cream and blend well.

Pour sauce over steaks and serve at once.

Steak au Poivre

Herb and Spice Steaks

6 servings

½ cup	(*125 mL*) oil
1 cup	(*250 mL*) cider vinegar
⅓ cup	(*80 mL*) brown sugar
2	garlic cloves, minced
¾ cup	(*180 mL*) minced onion
¼ tsp	(*1 mL*) cayenne pepper
¼ tsp	(*1 mL*) salt
½ tsp	(*3 mL*) marjoram
½ tsp	(*3 mL*) rosemary
6	8 oz (*225 g*) New York strip loin steaks

Heat the oil, vinegar, sugar, garlic, onions and seasonings together. Boil for 2 minutes. Remove from heat. Cool.

Place steaks in a deep pan. Pour the cool marinade over the steaks.

Refrigerate for 6 to 8 hours or overnight. Remove steaks and broil to your liking.

Steak Diane

8 servings

⅓ cup	(*80 mL*) butter
8	4 oz (*115 g*) filet steaks
4 oz	(*115 g*) mushrooms, sliced
2	green onions, minced
¼ cup	(*60 mL*) brandy
1½ cups	(*375 mL*) demi-glace (see *Sauces*)
¼ cup	(*60 mL*) sherry
¼ cup	(*60 mL*) heavy cream

In a large skillet, heat the butter. Fry the steaks in the butter 3½ to 4 minutes on each side. Remove and keep hot.

Add the mushrooms to the skillet; sauté until tender.

Add the green onions and sauté for 1 minute.

Carefully flame with brandy. Add the demi-glace, sherry and cream. Reduce to ¾ volume.

Pour sauce over steaks. Serve.

Filet Oscar

6 servings

3 tbsp	(*45 mL*) butter
6	6 oz (*170 g*) tenderloin steaks
8 oz	(*225 g*) crab meat
12	asparagus, blanched 5 minutes
6 tbsp	(*90 mL*) Béarnaise sauce (see *Sauces*)

Heat the butter and sauté the steaks to desired doneness.

Place on a baking sheet; top with crab meat and asparagus.

Place 1 tbsp (*15 mL*) of sauce on top of each steak and broil for 30 seconds or until sauce browns.

Tournedos Rossini

6 servings

¼ cup	(*60 mL*) butter
6	4 oz (*115 g*) filet steaks
12 oz	(*340 g*) pâté
¼ cup	(*60 mL*) flour
6	3-in. (*7 cm*) round croutons
1 cup	(*250 mL*) demi-glace (see *Sauces*)
¼ cup	(*60 mL*) sherry
¼ cup	(*60 mL*) heavy cream

Heat the butter in a skillet. Fry the steaks 3½ to 4 minutes on each side.

Remove to a hot platter.

Slice the pâté into rounds a little smaller than the steaks.

Dust with flour, and fry 1 minute each side in the butter.

Place the steaks on a crouton. Top with pâté.

Heat the demi-glace in a saucepan.

Add the sherry; reduce to half. Add the cream; simmer 1 minute.

Pour sauce over steaks. Serve.

NOTE : Classic Tournedos Rossini should be topped with a slice of truffle. But this is far too expensive in North America - about $60 an ounce!

Sauté lightly for 3 minutes. Chop the spinach. Add it to the skillet with the breadcrumbs, basil and broth.

Spread over steak. Sprinkle with cheese and cashews. Roll like a jelly roll. Tie with string every two inches. Bake, covered, in oven, for 2 hours.

Slice in 1-in. (*2,5 cm*) servings.

Swiss Steak

6 servings

¼ cup	(*60 mL*) oil
2	garlic cloves, minced
1	onion, sliced
1	green pepper, sliced
4 oz	(*115 g*) mushrooms, sliced
½ cup	(*125 mL*) flour
2¼ lbs	(*1 kg*) round steak, tenderized
2 tsp	(*10 mL*) salt
¼ tsp	(*1 mL*) pepper
½ tsp	(*3 mL*) basil
½ tsp	(*3 mL*) thyme
2 cups	(*500 mL*) tomato purée
1 cup	(*250 mL*) tomatoes, seeded and chopped

Heat oil in a large skillet.

Sauté garlic, onion, green pepper and mushrooms until tender.

Flour the meat. Brown in the oil with the vegetables. Add the seasonings, tomato purée and tomatoes.

Cover and simmer for 1½ hours over low heat.

Flank Steak Florentine

Flank Steak Florentine

6 servings

2¼ lbs	(*1 kg*) flank steak
3 tbsp	(*45 mL*) butter
1	small onion, diced
1	garlic clove, minced
2 oz	(*30 g*) mushrooms, sliced
10 oz	(*284 g*) spinach
1½ cups	(*375 mL*) breadcrumbs
1 tsp	(*5 mL*) basil
½ cup	(*125 mL*) chicken broth or white wine
1½ cups	(*375 mL*) grated Cheddar
¼ cup	(*60 mL*) cashews

Preheat oven to 350°F (*180°C*). Pound the steak on both sides with a mallet.

In a large skillet, heat the butter. Add the onion, garlic and mushrooms.

Filet de Boeuf Wellington

8 servings

Pastry

2 cups	*(500 mL)* flour
¾ tsp	*(4 mL)* salt
½ lb	*(225 g)* butter
⅓ cup	*(80 mL)* ice water

Beef

4 ½ lbs	*(2 kg)* tenderloin filet
3 tbsp	*(45 mL)* butter
1	onion, diced
4 oz	*(115 g)* mushrooms, quartered
1 lb	*(450 g)* liver pâté

Sauce

2 cups	*(500 mL)* demi-glace (see *Sauces*)
¼ cup	*(60 mL)* sherry
½ cup	*(125 mL)* heavy cream
2 tsp	*(10 mL)* green peppercorns

*Pastry : Sift the flour and salt into a bowl. Cut in ¾ of the butter. Add the water. Mix into walnut size pieces. Cover and chill for 20 minutes.

Uncover and roll out on a flour-dusted board. Dot with remaining butter. Fold into thirds.

Cover and refrigerate another 20 minutes.

Gather roasted beef filet, pâté and onion/mushroom mixture (duxelles). Roll out the dough for final rolling.

Spread pâté over pastry, then spread duxelles over pâté.

Lay the filet over the duxelles and carefully wrap the pastry around the filet.

Bake in oven for 25 minutes or until pastry is golden brown.

(Continued on next page)

Uncover. Roll out. Fold into thirds and refrigerate at least 3 more times. Refrigerate before final use. (*You may prefer to use 1 lb (450 g) of commercial puff pastry, instead.*)

Assembly : Roast the filet in a 425°F (*220°C*) oven for 20 minutes. Allow to cool.
Heat the butter in a skillet. Add the onion and mushrooms and sauté until all the liquid has evaporated. Scrape into a blender and blend on low for 20 seconds. (*This is a duxelles*).
Roll out the dough for the final rolling. Spread pâté over pastry.

Spread duxelles over pâté. Lay the filet over the duxelles.

Carefully wrap the pastry around the filet. Seal the edges. Decorate with remaining pastry.

Place filet, sealed side down, on a pastry sheet. Bake in preheated 425°F (*220°C*) oven 25 minutes or until pastry is golden brown. Let stand 5 minutes before serving.

Sauce : Pour demi-glace into a saucepan. Add sherry and reduce volume by half.

Add cream and simmer 5 minutes. Add the peppercorns. Pour into a serving bowl. Serve with beef.

Rib Roast of Beef

Rib Roast of Beef

8 servings

¼ cup	(*60 mL*) flour
2 tbsp	(*30 mL*) dry mustard
1 tsp	(*5 mL*) oregano
1 tsp	(*5 mL*) basil
½ tsp	(*3 mL*) thyme
½ tsp	(*3 mL*) salt

4½ lb	(*2 kg*) rib roast
2 tbsp	(*30 mL*) Worcestershire sauce
1	onion, chopped
2	carrots, chopped
2	celery stalks, chopped
1	bay leaf
1 cup	(*250 mL*) red wine
1 cup	(*250 mL*) water

Preheat oven to 325°F (*160°C*). Mix the flour, mustard and seasonings together.

Rub into roast. Place roast in pan. Pour over the Worcestershire sauce.

Surround the roast with the vegetables, bay leaf and pour in the wine and water. Place in oven.

Bake to desired doneness. Use juices to baste the roast.

Use juices to make a pan gravy for roast.

Pot-au-Feu

6 servings

2¼ lb	(1 kg)	shoulder roast
12 cups	(3 L)	water
1 tsp	(5 mL)	salt
1		carrot, sliced
1		turnip, diced
1		onion, sliced
1		parsnip, diced
2		celery stalks, diced
2		small zucchini, diced
1		cabbage, quartered
1		bouquet garni*

Have the meat tied together. Place in a large pot. Add water and salt. Cover and simmer for 2 hours.

Add the vegetables, (except the cabbage) and the bouquet garni.

Simmer for an additional 1½ hours.

Add the cabbage and continue to simmer another ½ hour. Discard the bouquet garni.

Serve the meat and vegetables with a little of the broth.

A bouquet garni is : thyme, marjoram, peppercorns, bay leaf and parsley, tied together in a cheesecloth.

Deli Corned Beef

8 servings

4 cups	(1 L)	water
1¼ cups	(310 mL)	salt
3 tbsp	(45 mL)	pickling spice
1 tsp	(5 mL)	saltpeter
1 tsp	(5 mL)	sugar
6		bay leaves
12		garlic cloves
4½ lbs	(2 kg)	beef brisket
1		onion
1		celery stalk
4 cups	(1 L)	water
1 tbsp	(15 mL)	prepared mustard
¼ cup	(60 mL)	brown sugar

Mix 4 cups (1 L) water with the seasonings; bring to a boil. Allow to cool.

Place brisket in a large crock or pan. Pour mixture over brisket. Arrange so that the brisket remains completely covered with brine. Cover with tin foil and refrigerate for 7 days.

Drain and rinse the brisket. Place brisket in a large pot or Dutch oven.

Add the onion and celery. Pour in 4 cups (1 L) water. Bring to a boil.

Reduce heat to a simmer. Simmer for 3 hours. Cool for 30 minutes in liquid.

Remove to a pastry sheet. Brush with mustard. Sprinkle with brown sugar.

Bake in a 350°F (180°C) oven for 30 minutes. Slice and serve.

Boiled Beef

6 servings

2¼ lbs	(1 kg)	beef brisket
2		leeks, washed and trimmed
1		bouquet garni
1		carrot, pared and chopped
1		onion, halved
1		celery stalk, chopped
1 tsp	(5 mL)	salt
8 cups	(2 L)	boiling water
12		small new potatoes
24		baby carrots

In a large pot or Dutch oven, place the brisket, leeks, bouquet garni, carrot, onion, celery and salt.

Pour in the boiling water. Bring to a boil. Reduce to low and simmer for 3 hours.

Remove any grease or scum as it floats to the top. Add the potatoes and baby carrots. Simmer for 40 more minutes.

Place brisket on a serving platter.

Surround with potatoes and carrots. Serve with horseradish, if desired.

Chef K's Fire Chili

8 servings

2¼ lbs	(*1 kg*) boneless lean beef, diced
¼ cup	(*60 mL*) oil
1	onion, sliced thin
1	green pepper, diced coarse
4 oz	(*115 g*) mushrooms, halved
2	garlic cloves, minced
4 cups	(*1 L*) tomatoes, seeded, peeled and chopped
2 tsp	(*10 mL*) salt
1 tsp	(*5 mL*) cayenne pepper
½ tsp	(*3 mL*) black pepper
2 tbsp	(*30 mL*) chili powder
2	10 oz (*284 mL*) cans kidney beans, drained

Trim the fat from the meat. Heat the oil in a large skillet. Sauté the onion, green pepper, mushrooms and garlic until tender. Add beef and brown over medium heat.

Drain excess grease. Add the tomatoes. Stir in the seasonings. Cover and simmer for 1 hour. Add beans and simmer for 10 minutes. Serve.

Chef K's Fire Chili

Old-Fashioned Beef Stew

6 servings

2¼ lbs	(*1 kg*) stewing beef
¼ cup	(*60 mL*) oil
4	potatoes, diced
1	onion, sliced thin
2	celery stalks
2	carrots, diced
8 oz	(*225 g*) button mushrooms
3 cups	(*750 mL*) beef stock
¼ cup	(*60 mL*) tomato paste
1 tsp	(*5 mL*) salt
½ tsp	(*3 mL*) black pepper
½ tsp	(*3 mL*) basil
½ tsp	(*3 mL*) paprika
1 tsp	(*5 mL*) Worcestershire sauce
1 tbsp	(*15 mL*) soya sauce

Trim the fat from the beef. Heat the oil in a pot or Dutch oven.

Add the potatoes, onion, celery, carrots, mushrooms and sauté for 3 minutes. Add the beef and brown. Add the beef stock, tomato paste, seasonings, Worcestershire and soya sauces. Bring to a boil.

Reduce and simmer for 3 hours. Serve.

English Steak and Kidney Pie

8 servings

Pastry

2 cups	(500 mL)	flour
¾ tsp	(4 mL)	salt
½ lb	(225 g)	butter
⅓ cup	(80 mL)	ice water

Filling

1 tsp	(5 mL)	salt
pinch		pepper
1 tsp	(5 mL)	thyme
½ cup	(125 mL)	flour
2¼ lbs	(1 kg)	rump steak, cut into thin 1½ in. (4 cm) wide strips
¼ cup	(60 mL)	chopped bacon
2		onions, chopped
4 oz	(115 g)	mushrooms, sliced
2 ½ cups	(625 mL)	beef broth
3		veal kidneys
2		egg yolks

*Pastry : Sift together the flour and salt into a bowl. Put ¾ of the butter into the flour.

Add the water and mix into walnut size pieces. Cover and chill 20 minutes. Uncover and roll out to ⅛ in. (0,5 cm) on a flour-dusted board. Dot with the remaining butter. Fold into thirds.

Cover and refrigerate for an additional 20 minutes. Uncover.

Roll out and fold into thirds. Refrigerate for 20 minutes. Repeat this process at least 3 more times.

Filling : Blend the seasonings into the flour. Dust the beef with seasoned flour.

Heat the bacon in a large skillet. Brown the beef in the bacon over high heat. Add the onions and mushrooms and sauté for 3 minutes.

Pour the beef broth into the skillet. Cover and simmer for 1½ hours.

Clean the kidneys. Using a sharp paring knife, remove the membranes. Slice the kidneys thin.

Preheat oven to 375°F (190°C).

Pour the beef mixture into a large casserole dish, 9 x 12 in. (23 x 30 cm).

Stir in the kidneys. Dampen the edges of the pan. Roll out the pastry.

Place on top and seal the edges. Cut a hole ½ in. (1,2 cm) in diameter in the center.

Roll a small piece of tin foil into a tube and place in hole.

Cut remaining pastry into designs and decorate.

Brush with egg yolk. Bake in oven for 50 minutes or until golden brown.

Beef Bordelaise

6 servings

⅓ cup	(80 mL)	butter
2¼ lbs	(1 kg)	round steak, cut in thin 1-in. (2,5 cm) wide strips
4 oz	(115 g)	button mushrooms
¼ cup	(60 mL)	chopped shallots
½ cup	(125 mL)	Bordeaux wine
2 cups	(500 mL)	Espagnole Sauce (see *Sauces*)
2 tbsp	(30 mL)	beef marrow, chopped fine
1 tbsp	(15 mL)	chopped parsley

In a large skillet, heat the butter. Fast fry the beef strips.

Remove and keep hot.

Add the mushrooms and shallots. Sauté for 3 minutes.

Add the wine and reduce to one third.

Add the sauce, marrow, parsley and simmer two minutes.

Pour over beef strips. Serve.

*Or use 1 lb (450 g) of puff pastry.

Beef and Cheese Goulash

8 servings

1½ lbs	(675 g) egg noodles
2¼ lbs	(1 kg) cooked beef, cut into ¾-in. (2 cm) cubes
¼ cup	(60 mL) butter
3	onions, chopped
3 cups	(750 mL) tomato sauce
1½ tsp	(8 mL) paprika
1 tsp	(5 mL) salt
¼ tsp	(1 mL) pepper
1 tbsp	(15 mL) caraway seeds
1 cup	(250 mL) grated Colby cheese
1 cup	(250 mL) grated Caraway cheese

Preheat oven to 375°F (190°C).

Cook noodles in a large pot of boiling, salted water, about 8-10 minutes or until al dente (*tender but firm*). Drain well.

Place noodles in a greased 13 x 9 in. (*33 x 23 cm*) baking dish. Top with beef.

Melt the butter; sauté the onions over low heat until tender.

Add the tomato sauce and seasonings; simmer 15 minutes. Pour sauce over the beef.

Sprinkle with caraway seeds and cheeses.

Bake in oven for 30 minutes or until cheese has melted and is lightly browned.

Pepper Steak

Pepper Steak

4 servings

1½ lbs	(675 g) round steak, cut into small strips
½ cup	(125 mL) flour
3 tbsp	(45 mL) oil
1	onion, sliced
1	green pepper, sliced
1	celery stalk, sliced
2 oz	(60 g) mushrooms
2	tomatoes, quartered
½ cup	(125 mL) beef broth
¼ cup	(60 mL) sherry
2 tbsp	(30 mL) soya sauce
1 tsp	(5 mL) Worcestershire sauce

Dust the beef with flour. Heat oil in a large skillet or wok.

Fast fry the beef to brown. Add the onion, green pepper, celery and sliced mushrooms. Fry for 2 minutes. Add the remaining ingredients. Cook for 2 more minutes.

Serve with rice.

Beef and Mushrooms with Old Cheddar

8 servings

4 cups	(*1 L*) cooked rice
2¼ lbs	(*1 kg*) cooked beef, cut in thin julienne strips
1 lb	(*450 g*) button mushrooms, sautéed in butter
¼ cup	(*60 mL*) butter
¼ cup	(*60 mL*) all-purpose flour
2 cups	(*500 mL*) Espagnole Sauce (see *Sauces*)
2 cups	(*500 mL*) heavy cream
1 tbsp	(*15 mL*) green peppercorns
3 cups	(*750 mL*) grated old Cheddar cheese
¼ cup	(*60 mL*) breadcrumbs

Preheat over to 400°F (*200°C*).

Spread the rice in the bottom of a greased 13 x 9 in. (*33 x 23 cm*) baking dish.

Cover with beef strips and sautéed mushrooms.

Melt butter over medium heat; stir in flour.

Add Espagnole Sauce and cream; heat, stirring constantly, until mixture thickens and comes to a boil. Stir in green peppercorns. Pour sauce over meat mixture.

Combine cheese and breadcrumbs and sprinkle over sauce.

Bake in oven for 25 minutes or until heated through.

Beef Stroganoff

8 servings

2¼ lbs	(*1 kg*) round steak
¼ cup	(*60 mL*) oil
3 tbsp	(*45 mL*) butter
1	celery stalk, sliced
1	onion, sliced
1	green pepper, sliced
½ lb	(*225 g*) mushrooms, sliced
⅓ cup	(*80 mL*) flour
1¼ cups	(*300 mL*) beef stock
¾ cup	(*180 mL*) sherry
2 tbsp	(*30 mL*) Worcestershire sauce
2 tbsp	(*30 mL*) prepared mustard
¼ cup	(*60 mL*) tomato paste
1	bay leaf
2 tsp	(*10 mL*) paprika
½ tsp	(*3 mL*) thyme
¼ tsp	(*1 mL*) pepper
1 cup	(*250 mL*) sour cream
4 cups	(*1 L*) cooked egg noodles, hot

Cut the steak into slices.

Heat the oil and the butter. Brown the beef, then sauté the vegetables until tender. Add the flour and stir for 2 minutes.

Add the beef stock, sherry, Worcestershire sauce, mustard, tomato paste and seasonings.

Cover and simmer for 1¼ hours.

Add sour cream and mix thoroughly. Pour over noodles and serve.

Beef Bourguignon

8-10 servings

4½ lbs	(*2 kg*) chuck beef, cubed
1 tsp	(*5 mL*) dry mustard
1 tsp	(*5 mL*) basil
1 tbsp	(*15 mL*) salt
½ tsp	(*3 mL*) pepper
½ lb	(*225 g*) bacon
20	pearl onions
2 cups	(*500 mL*) red wine
1 cup	(*250 mL*) sherry
1	bay leaf
¼ cup	(*60 mL*) chopped parsley
1 tsp	(*5 mL*) thyme
1 lb	(*450 g*) mushrooms, sliced
3 tbsp	(*45 mL*) flour
¼ cup	(*60 mL*) water

Season the beef with the mustard, basil, salt and pepper.

In a Dutch oven, sauté the bacon. Remove the bacon pieces.

Brown the beef in the fat. Add onions and sauté until tender. Add wine, sherry, bay leaf, parsley and thyme. Cover and simmer for 2 hours.

Add the mushrooms and simmer another 30 minutes.

Mix the flour with water into a very smooth paste.

Add to the beef and simmer, while stirring, for 5 minutes or until mixture thickens.

Serve with new potatoes.

Beef Stroganoff

Filet Oscar Crêpes

8 servings

1	small onion, finely chopped
	margarine
3 cups	(*750 mL*) sliced mushrooms
1 lb	(*450 g*) beef tenderloin
	salt and pepper
16	asparagus spears
8	8-in. (*20 cm*) crêpes
1 cup	(*250 mL*) grated Swiss cheese
1 cup	(*250 mL*) cooked baby shrimp
1 cup	(*250 mL*) Béarnaise sauce (see *Sauces*)

Sauté onion in small amount of margarine over medium heat until tender. Set aside. Sauté mushrooms in additional margarine over high heat until tender; set aside.

Cut beef into thin slivers and sauté to desired doneness. Return onions and mushrooms to pan, reheat, and season to taste.

Meanwhile, cook asparagus in boiling, salted water just until tender, about 3 minutes; drain.

Spoon meat mixture onto each crêpe, sprinkle with cheese, and roll. Place on a baking sheet. Top with shrimp, 2 asparagus spears, and Béarnaise sauce.

Place under heated broiler until sauce is slightly browned, about 1 minute.

Filet Oscar Crêpes

Texan Short Ribs

8 servings

4 ½ lbs	(*2 kg*) short ribs, cut into 3-in. (*7 cm*) pieces
3 tbsp	(*45 mL*) oil
⅓ cup	(*80 mL*) flour
1	onion, chopped
2 tsp	(*10 mL*) salt
½ tsp	(*3 mL*) pepper
½ tsp	(*3 mL*) oregano
½ tsp	(*3 mL*) thyme
½ tsp	(*3 mL*) paprika
¼ cup	(*60 mL*) boiling water
2 cups	(*500 mL*) chili sauce
⅓ cup	(*80 mL*) diced pickles

Trim excess fat from ribs. Heat the oil in a large pot or Dutch oven. Dust the ribs with flour, then brown in oil. Drain excess fat, reserving about 1 tbsp (*15 mL*). Add the onion and fry to brown. Sprinkle with seasonings. Add water and reduce heat. Cover and simmer for 1½ hours.

Add the chili sauce and pickles. Simmer for 1 hour more or until ribs are very tender.

Serve with rice pilaf of your choice.

Steak Tartare

4 servings

1 lb	*(450 g)* tenderloin
½ cup	*(125 g)* finely chopped green onions
1 tsp	*(5 mL)* minced garlic
2 tbsp	*(30 mL)* sherry
½ tsp	*(3 mL)* cracked pepper
1 tsp	*(5 mL)* chopped parsley
1 tsp	*(5 mL)* salt
1 tsp	*(5 mL)* Worcestershire sauce
1 tbsp	*(15 mL)* brandy
1 tsp	*(5 mL)* capers
4	egg yolks
1	pumpernickel bread

Grind the tenderloin twice.

Place the meat in a bowl, add onions and blend.

Blend in the garlic, sherry, pepper, parsley, salt, Worcestershire sauce, brandy and capers.

Divide into four servings and place on plates.

Make an indentation in the center of each portion. Place an egg yolk in the indentation.

Serve with pumpernickel.

Place ground meat in a bowl, add green onions and blend.

Blend in the garlic, sherry, pepper, parsley, salt, Worcestershire sauce, brandy and capers.

Divide meat mixture into four servings and place on plates. Make an indentation in the center of each portion.

Place an egg yolk in the indentation.

Meatball Soup

8 servings

Meatballs

1 lb	(*450 g*) extra lean ground beef
1 tsp	(*5 mL*) Worcestershire sauce
⅓ cup	(*80 mL*) breadcrumbs
¼ cup	(*60 mL*) milk
1	egg, beaten
¼ tsp	(*1 mL*) garlic powder
¼ tsp	(*1 mL*) oregano
¼ tsp	(*1 mL*) thyme
¼ tsp	(*1 mL*) basil
pinch	chili powder
½ tsp	(*3 mL*) paprika
1 tsp	(*5 mL*) salt
¼ tsp	(*1 mL*) pepper

Preheat oven to 350°F (*180°C*). Combine the beef, Worcestershire sauce and breadcrumbs together.

Beat the egg with the milk and add the seasonings. Blend into meat mixture.

Bake in oven for 12 to 15 minutes. Drain excess fat and reserve.

Soup

¼ cup	(*60 mL*) oil
1	onion, sliced
1	green pepper, sliced
4 oz	(*115 g*) mushrooms, sliced
2	garlic cloves, minced
2	celery stalks, sliced
4 cups	(*1 L*) chopped tomatoes
2 cups	(*500 mL*) chicken broth
½ cup	(*125 mL*) vermicelli, broken
1 tsp	(*5 mL*) salt
1 tsp	(*5 mL*) oregano
¼ tsp	(*1 mL*) pepper
¼ cup	(*60 mL*) sherry

In a pot or Dutch oven, heat the oil. Add the onion, green pepper, mushrooms, garlic and celery; sauté until tender.

Add the tomatoes and broth; bring to a boil. Add the vermicelli and reduce to a simmer.

Simmer, covered, for 15 minutes. Add the seasonings, sherry and meatballs.

Simmer 5 more minutes. Serve.

Shepherd's Pie

4 servings

3 tbsp	(*45 mL*) oil
2	onions, minced
2	celery stalks, minced
2	carrots, finely diced
1 lb	(*450 g*) lean ground beef
½ tsp	(*3 mL*) savory
1 tsp	(*5 mL*) salt
10 oz	(*284 mL*) can creamed corn
4 cups	(*1 L*) mashed potatoes

Preheat oven to 375°F (*190°C*).

Heat the oil in a skillet. Sauté the onions, celery and carrots.

Add the beef and brown. Season with savory and salt. Drain excess fat.

Place the meat mixture in a casserole dish.

Pour the corn over the meat. Top with mashed potatoes.

Bake in oven for 20 minutes.

Cheese Burger Insane

8 servings

2¼ lbs	(*1 kg*) lean ground beef
2 tsp	(*10 mL*) seasoned salt
pinch	pepper
1	egg
¼ cup	(*60 mL*) fine dry breadcrumbs
8	slices Havarti or medium Cheddar cheese, about 1 in. (*2,5 cm*) square and ¼ in. (*0,5 cm*) thick

Combine ground beef, seasonings, egg and breadcrumbs; mix thoroughly.

Divide into 8 portions. From each portion, make 2 thin patties. Sandwich 1 cheese slice between the patties and pinch edges to seal. Place under heated broiler and cook until browned, about 6 minutes per side. Serve on fresh buns, garnished with your favorite fixin's.

Ground Sirloin Wellington

8 servings

Pastry

2½ cups	(*625 mL*) flour
1 tsp	(*5 mL*) salt
¾ cup	(*180 mL*) butter, chilled and diced
1	egg
½ cup	(*125 mL*) sour cream

Ground Sirloin Wellington

Filling

¼ cup	(*60 mL*) butter
4 oz	(*115 g*) mushrooms
¼ cup	(*60 mL*) minced onion
2¼ lbs	(*1 kg*) twice-ground sirloin
1 tbsp	(*15 mL*) parsley
1 tbsp	(*15 mL*) basil
1 tsp	(*5 mL*) salt
1 tsp	(*5 mL*) pepper
2	eggs
8 oz	(*225 g*) liver pâté

Pastry : Sift together the flour and salt. Mix in the butter until pastry is in large coarse pieces.

Mix egg with the sour cream. Blend this mixture into the flour. Mix into a smooth ball. Cover and chill 1 hour.

Preheat oven at 350°F (*180°C*).

Filling : Melt the butter and sauté the mushrooms and onion. Allow to cool. Mix the sirloin with the mushrooms, onion, seasonings and eggs. Roll out the pastry in 8 rectangles of 8 x 5 in. (*20 x 12 cm*). Spread the pâté in the center then add the filling. Wrap the meat and seal the edges. Brush with a little melted butter.

Bake for 1 hour, or until pastry is golden brown in color.

Java Beef

8 servings

2 tbsp	(*30 mL*) butter
1	onion, sliced
1	green pepper, sliced
1½ lbs	(*675 g*) lean ground beef
1 tsp	(*5 mL*) salt
1 tbsp	(*15 mL*) curry powder
½ cup	(*125 mL*) raisins
½ cup	(*125 mL*) dried, chopped apricots
1 cup	(*250 mL*) cashews
1 cup	(*250 mL*) beef stock
2 cups	(*500 mL*) peas, fresh or frozen
½ cup	(*125 mL*) chopped pimiento

Melt the butter and sauté the onion and green pepper.

Add the beef, salt and curry powder; brown. Blend in the raisins, apricots and cashews. Add the beef stock and simmer for 20 minutes.

Add the peas and pimiento. Simmer an additional 10 minutes.
Serve with rice and chutney on the side.

Java Beef

Old-Fashioned Chili 'n Cheese

8 servings

2	garlic cloves, minced
1	medium onion, chopped
2 tbsp	(*30 mL*) vegetable oil
1 lb	(*450 g*) lean ground beef
28 oz	(*796 mL*) can tomatoes
2½ cups	(*625 mL*) water
2	tomatoes, peeled, seeded and chopped
1	green pepper, chopped
2 tbsp	(*30 mL*) chili powder
1 tbsp	(*15 mL*) paprika
1 tsp	(*5 mL*) rubbed thyme
½ tsp	(*3 mL*) dried oregano leaves
½ tsp	(*3 mL*) dried basil leaves
½ tsp	(*3 mL*) cayenne pepper
1 tsp	(*5 mL*) salt
14 oz	(*398 mL*) can kidney beans, rinsed
½ cup	(*125 mL*) grated old Cheddar cheese
½ cup	(*125 mL*) grated Swiss cheese

(Continued on next page)

Meat Loaf with Mushroom Sauce

1 tsp	(5 mL) basil
1½ tsp	(8 mL) salt
½ tsp	(3 mL) pepper
4	strips bacon

Preheat oven to 350°F (180°C). Combine the beef with the eggs, breadcrumbs and seasonings. Shape into a 9 x 5 in. (22 x 12 cm) loaf pan. Lay the bacon across the top.

Bake in oven for 1¼ to 1½ hours.

Sauce

3 tbsp	(45 mL) butter
8 oz	(225 g) mushrooms, sliced
3 tbsp	(45 mL) flour
1 cup	(250 mL) heavy cream
2 cups	(500 mL) beef stock
¼ cup	(60 mL) sherry
¼ cup	(60 mL) tomato paste

In a saucepan, heat the butter.

Sauté the mushrooms until tender.

Add the flour and cook for 2 minutes.

Add the cream, stock and sherry. Stir.

Reduce heat and simmer until thickened. Whisk in tomato paste.

Pour over meat loaf.

Sauté garlic and onion in oil until tender. Stir in ground beef and continue cooking until no pink remains; drain.

Stir in canned tomatoes, water, fresh tomatoes, green pepper, seasonings and kidney beans. Bring to a boil; reduce heat and simmer 2 ½ to 3 hours.

At serving time, spoon chili into individual bowls and sprinkle with cheese. Serve with garlic bread.

Meat Loaf with Mushroom Sauce

6 servings

Loaf

2¼ lbs	(1 kg) extra lean ground beef
2	eggs
⅔ cup	(160 mL) fine breadcrumbs
¼ cup	(60 mL) chopped parsley

Poultry

Chicken is such a wonderfully versatile item that the number of ways for preparing it is truly limitless. And even when the bones are picked clean, they can be used to create endlessly useful stocks and soup bases.

Little wonder, then, that the most famous cooking school in the world is not named after a great chef, but after a world-famous chicken dish — Cordon Bleu.

But extraordinary as this bird is, there is more to poultry than chicken alone. The category includes any domesticated bird used for human consumption, including turkey, duck, goose and Cornish hens.

You can also include game birds, such as pheasant and partridge, in the poultry category.

Poultry can be cooked using most cookery methods. Experiment with them all and you will find a never-ending menu would be possible from poultry alone.

Roasting Timetable at 325°F (160°C)		
	Weight	Time
Chicken	2-3 lbs (1 kg)	1¼-1½ hrs
	4-5 lbs (2 kg)	2-2½ hrs
	5-6 lbs (3 kg)	2½-3 hrs
	6-7 lbs (4 kg)	3-3½ hrs
Turkey	6-8 lbs (3-4 kg)	3-4 hrs
	8-12 lbs (4-6 kg)	4-5 hrs
	12-16 lbs (6-8 kg)	5-6 hrs
	16-20 lbs (8 à 9 kg)	6-7½ hrs

Test for Doneness: It is best to use a meat thermometer, inserted in the thigh, but not touching the bone. Poultry is cooked when the temperature reads 190°F (87°C).

Without a thermometer, you can tell if the bird is done when the leg moves freely in its socket, and when the juices run clear rather than pink when you stab the thickest part of the thigh.

Peach and Mango Chicken

4-6 servings

2 ½ - 3 lb	*(1,1 - 1,4 kg)* fryer chicken
¼ cup	*(60 mL)* butter
1 cup	*(250 mL)* diced mangos
½ cup	*(125 mL)* diced peaches
3	strips lemon rind
1¼ cups	*(310 mL)* chicken stock
1 tbsp	*(15 mL)* lemon juice
½ cup	*(125 mL)* heavy cream
	salt and pepper

Preheat oven to 350°F *(180°C)*.

Fry the chicken in the butter until browned on all sides. Add mangos, peaches, lemon rind and chicken stock.

Cover and bake in oven for 1 hour.

Remove chicken from pan and keep warm.

Remove lemon rind. Add lemon juice and cream. Season to taste.

Bring sauce to a simmer and reduce until thickened.

Pour sauce over chicken and serve.

Peach and Mango Chicken

Rosemary Roast Chicken

4 servings

2¼ lb	*(1 kg)* fryer chicken
1 tbsp	*(15 mL)* melted butter
¼ tsp	*(1 mL)* salt
pinch	pepper
pinch	paprika
1 tbsp	*(15 mL)* rosemary

Preheat oven to 325°F *(160°C)*.

Stuff chicken if you choose. Use your favorite stuffing.

Place chicken in a roasting pan. Brush with melted butter. Sprinkle with seasonings. Roast in oven for 60 minutes.

(If you use a stuffing, a little longer cooking time may be required.)

Chicken with Espagnole Sauce

4 servings

3 lbs	(1,4 kg) chicken pieces
¼ cup	(60 mL) vegetable oil
	salt and pepper
	paprika
	dried oregano leaves
	rubbed thyme
¼ cup	(60 mL) brandy
½ cup	(125 mL) heavy cream
¼ cup	(60 mL) sherry
5 tbsp	(75 mL) all-purpose flour
½ cup	(125 mL) Espagnole Sauce (see *Sauces*)
1⅓ cups	(330 mL) grated mild Cheddar cheese

Preheat oven to 350°F (*180°C*).

Brown the chicken in oil, about 5 minutes, then transfer to a baking dish.

Sprinkle lightly with seasonings and bake in oven for 45 minutes or until cooked through. Drain fat, pour brandy over and flame.

Remove chicken from pan and keep warm.

Combine cream and sherry; stir in flour until smooth.

Pour cream mixture and Espagnole Sauce into pan juices; cook and stir until thickened. Add the cheese; stir just until melted.

Transfer chicken pieces to a serving dish and pour sauce over.

Southern Fried Chicken Marylands

8 servings

2¼ lbs	(1 kg) chicken marylands*
1 tbsp	(15 mL) salt
1 tbsp	(15 mL) paprika
1 tsp	(5 mL) each : oregano, thyme, sage, basil, garlic powder, black pepper, onion powder, marjoram
4 cups	(1 L) fine breadcrumbs
4	eggs
½ cup	(125 mL) milk
2 cups	(500 mL) flour
3 cups	(750 mL) oil

Preheat oven to 350°F (*180°C*).

Wash the chicken and pat dry. Mix the seasonings in the breadcrumbs. Mix the eggs in the milk.

Dust chicken with flour. Dip in egg mixture. Roll in seasoned breadcrumbs.

Heat oil to 325°F (*160°C*). Fry chicken in oil until golden brown. Remove from oil and place in paper towels to soak excess oil.

Place on baking sheet and bake in oven 12 to 15 minutes.

* A maryland is the leg and thigh of a chicken left whole.

Chicken Sauté Chasseur

4 servings

1	fryer chicken, cut into 8 pieces
1½ tbsp	(22 mL) butter
1½ tbsp	(22 mL) oil
¼ cup	(60 mL) sweet white wine
⅔ cup	(160 mL) Chasseur Sauce
1 tbsp	(15 mL) chopped parsley

Sauté the chicken in the butter and oil.

Once cooked, remove from heat and keep warm.

Add the wine and reduce by half. Add the sauce and simmer 5 minutes.

Pour over chicken and sprinkle with parsley.

Serve.

Chicken Sauternes Véronique

Chicken Sauternes Véronique

8 servings

2	fryer chickens, cut into quarters
2 tbsp	(*30 mL*) melted butter
1 tbsp	(*15 mL*) sugar
	salt and white pepper

Preheat oven to 350°F (*180 °C*).

Brush chicken with melted butter. Sprinkle with sugar, salt and pepper.

Bake in over for 45 minutes.

Sauce

3 tbsp	(*45 mL*) butter
3 tbsp	(*45 mL*) flour
½ cup	(*125 mL*) sauternes wine
½ cup	(*125 mL*) chicken stock
½ cup	(*125 mL*) light cream
2 cups	(*500 mL*) green grapes, halved

Sauce : In a saucepan, melt butter and add flour. Cook for 2 minutes without browning.

Add wine and chicken stock. Reduce to half.

Add cream and simmer until sauce thickens. Add grapes.

Place cooked chicken on a platter, pour sauce over chicken and serve.

Chicken Paprika

8 servings

½ cup	*(125 mL)*	flour
1 tbsp	*(15 mL)*	salt
1 tbsp	*(15 mL)*	paprika
1 tsp	*(5 mL)*	pepper
2		fryer chickens, cut into 8 pieces
⅓ cup	*(80 mL)*	oil
2½ cups	*(625 mL)*	chicken stock
1 cup	*(250 mL)*	sour cream

Mix the flour with the seasonings. Wash the chicken and coat with seasoned flour.

In a large skillet, heat the oil and brown the chicken. Add the chicken stock and simmer for 40 minutes.

Remove chicken and keep warm.

Swirl in the sour cream and simmer for 5 minutes.

Pour sauce over chicken and serve with buttered noodles.

Chicken Paprika

Polynesian Chicken

4 servings

1 tsp	*(5 mL)*	salt
1 tsp	*(5 mL)*	paprika
½ cup	*(125 mL)*	flour
2¼ lb	*(1 kg)*	fryer chicken, cut into 8 pieces
½ cup	*(250 mL)*	shortening
1 cup	*(250 mL)*	orange juice
2 tbsp	*(30 mL)*	brown sugar
2 tbsp	*(30 mL)*	vinegar
1 tsp	*(5 mL)*	basil
1 tsp	*(5 mL)*	ground nutmeg
1¼ cups	*(310 mL)*	sliced peaches

Combine salt, paprika and flour. Lightly coat chicken.

Heat shortening in a large skillet. Sauté chicken until golden brown on all sides.

Mix the orange juice, brown sugar, vinegar, basil and nutmeg in a bowl.

Add to chicken. Cover and simmer 35 to 40 minutes until chicken is tender.

Add peaches and simmer 5 more minutes. Serve.

Coq au Vin

8 servings

4 lb	(*1,8 kg*) chicken, cut into pieces
3 tbsp	(*45 mL*) flour
¼ cup	(*60 mL*) butter
½ cup	(*125 mL*) brandy
1 tsp	(*5 mL*) thyme
1 tsp	(*5 mL*) paprika
2 tsp	(*10 mL*) salt
1½ cups	(*375 mL*) dry red wine
1½ cups	(*375 mL*) strong chicken stock
4	slices bacon, diced
1 cup	(*250 mL*) pearl onions
1 cup	(*250 mL*) button mushrooms

Dust the chicken in the flour. Brown in butter over low heat. Flame with brandy.

Add seasonings, red wine and chicken stock. Cover and simmer until chicken is tender, about 40 minutes.

In a sauté pan, brown diced bacon and sauté the onions and mushrooms. Drain any oil.

Add to chicken 5 minutes before chicken is done.

1

Flame browned chicken with brandy.

2

Add seasonings, red wine and chicken stock. Cover and simmer until chicken is tender, about 40 minutes.

3

In a sauté pan, brown the diced bacon and sauté the onions and mushrooms.

4

Add to chicken 5 minutes before chicken is done.

Swiss Chicken

8 servings

8	boneless chicken breasts
	salt and pepper
	paprika
	vegetable oil
8 oz	(*225 g*) Black Forest ham, thinly sliced
16	cooked asparagus spears
8	slices Swiss cheese

Sprinkle the chicken breasts lightly with salt, pepper and paprika.

Sauté in vegetable oil over medium heat or grill until cooked through.

Top each breast with ham, 2 spears of asparagus, and a slice of cheese.

Place under a heated broiler just until cheese melts.

Serve immediately.

Chicken à la Nantua

8-10 servings

8-10		boneless chicken breasts
6 cups	(*1,5 L*) chicken stock or water
¾ lb	(*340 g*) cooked baby shrimp
1½ cups	(*375 mL*) crab meat
1 cup	(*250 mL*) Velouté Sauce (see *Sauces*)
2 cups	(*500 mL*) Supreme Sauce (see *Sauces*)
⅓ cup	(*80 mL*) grated Parmesan cheese

Preheat oven to 350°F (*180°C*).

Drop chicken breasts into simmering stock; simmer just until cooked through, about 10 minutes. Remove from stock and cover tightly.

Combine shrimp, crab meat, and Velouté Sauce; spoon into a greased shallow baking dish.

Place the poached breasts over the seafood mixture. Spoon Supreme Sauce over.

Sprinkle with Parmesan cheese and bake in oven until heated through and browned, about 15 minutes.

Three Pepper Chicken Breasts

6 servings

6	boneless chicken breasts, 6 oz (*170 g*) each
1 tbsp	(*15 mL*) fresh cracked black peppercorns
1 tbsp	(*15 mL*) green Madagascar peppercorns
1 tbsp	(*15 mL*) fresh cracked white peppercorns
3 tbsp	(*45 mL*) oil
2 cups	(*500 mL*) demi-glace (see *Sauces*)
¼ cup	(*60 mL*) heavy cream
¼ cup	(*60 mL*) sherry

Wash the chicken breasts.

Mix together the peppercorns and press into chicken, making sure to cover the entire chicken breast.

Heat the oil in a skillet. Sauté each breast in the oil, about 2½ minutes each side. Remove from oil and keep hot.

Add the demi-glace, cream and sherry. Simmer for 5 minutes.

Pour sauce over chicken and serve.

Mix the cornstarch with 1 tbsp (*15 mL*) water, add to sauce and bring back to a boil. Pour sauce over chicken.

Chicken Supremes en Papillote

6 servings

6	boneless chicken breasts, 6 oz (*170 g*) each
3 tbsp	(*45 mL*) butter
6	wax paper hearts, buttered
12	slices Black Forest ham, 1 oz (*30 g*) each
¾ cup	(*180 mL*) Italienne Sauce

Preheat oven to 425°F (*220°C*).

Brown the breasts in the butter. Remove and cool.

On one half of the paper heart, place a slice of ham and 1 tbsp (*15 mL*) of sauce on top of the ham.

Then top the ham with a breast. Add 1 tbsp (*15 mL*) of sauce then another slice of ham.

Fold the paper over to encase the chicken. Pleat the edge so that no air escapes during cooking.

Bake in oven until the papillotes puff up with air. Serve at once.

Lemon Chicken

Lemon Chicken

4 servings

3 tbsp	(*45 mL*) oil
4	boneless chicken breasts, 6 oz (*170 g*) each
1 tbsp	(*15 mL*) sesame seeds
2 tbsp	(*30 mL*) butter
¼ cup	(*60 mL*) sugar
¼ cup	(*60 mL*) water
¼ cup	(*60 mL*) lemon juice
2 tsp	(*10 mL*) cornstarch
1 tbsp	(*15 mL*) water

Heat the oil in a sauté pan.

Flatten the chicken breasts and sauté 2½ minutes each side. Top with sesame seeds. Remove and keep warm.

Melt the butter in a saucepan. Add the sugar. Stir constantly and cook until the sugar turns a caramel color.

Add ¼ cup (*60 mL*) water and lemon juice and bring to a boil.

Chicken Washington

6 servings

2 tbsp	(30 mL)	butter
¼ cup	(60 mL)	finely chopped mushrooms
2 tbsp	(30 mL)	flour
½ cup	(125 mL)	light cream
¼ tsp	(1 mL)	salt
pinch		cayenne pepper
1¼ cups	(310 mL)	grated old Cheddar cheese
6		boneless chicken breasts, 6 oz (170 g) each
¼ cup	(60 mL)	flour
2		eggs, slightly beaten
¾ cup	(180 mL)	fine breadcrumbs
½ cup	(125 mL)	shortening

In a saucepan, melt the butter. Sauté the mushrooms until tender.

Blend in the flour and stir until smooth. Add the cream, salt and pepper and simmer until thick. Stir in cheese and continue to stir until it melts. Remove from heat and chill 2 hours. Cut into six even pieces.

Preheat oven to 350°F (180°C).

While the filling chills, pound chicken breasts, then add filling to each and fold in two. Dust with flour, dip in eggs and roll in breadcrumbs.

Heat shortening and fry chicken enough to brown on each side.

Place on pastry sheet and bake 10 minutes in oven. Serve at once.

Chicken Sauté Cumberland

6 servings

6		boneless chicken breasts
2 tbsp	(30 mL)	butter
2 tbsp	(30 mL)	oil

Sauce

1 cup	(250 mL)	red currant jelly
1 tbsp	(15 mL)	grated orange rind
1 tbsp	(15 mL)	grated lemon rind
1 cup	(250 mL)	orange juice
¼ cup	(60 mL)	lemon juice
1½ tsp	(8 mL)	ginger
¼ cup	(60 mL)	sherry
1 tbsp	(15 mL)	Dijon mustard
1 tbsp	(15 mL)	cornstarch
2 tbsp	(30 mL)	water

Sauté the chicken in the butter and oil over medium-low heat until the meat is tender, about 8 minutes per side. Remove and keep warm.

In a saucepan, combine the jelly, orange and lemon rinds, juices, ginger, sherry and mustard. Bring to a gentle boil (coddle).

Mix the cornstarch with the water. Mix in sauce and simmer for 5 minutes or until sauce has thickened.

Place chicken on plate and cover with sauce.

Chicken Rombough

4 servings

4		boneless chicken breasts
6 oz	(170 g)	Brie cheese
16		medium-size shrimp
¼ cup	(60 mL)	crushed pineapple, drained
3 tbsp	(45 mL)	cashews
3 tbsp	(45 mL)	sultana raisins
2 tbsp	(30 mL)	melted butter
1 cup	(250 mL)	heavy cream
1 tbsp	(15 mL)	peach flavoring
2 tsp	(10 mL)	cornstarch
3 tbsp	(45 mL)	peach schnapps

Preheat oven to 350°F (180°C).

Pound the chicken flat. Place 1½ oz (45 g) of cheese, 4 shrimp, 1 tbsp (15 mL) of pineapple and a sprinkle of cashews and raisins on each breast.

Wrap the chicken around the filling. Brush with melted butter. Bake in oven 15 to 20 minutes.

Mix the cream with peach flavoring and heat to a boil.

Combine cornstarch with peach schnapps and add to cream. Simmer until thick.

Remove chicken from oven. Place on plates and cover with sauce.

Chicken Melba

6 servings

6	boneless chicken breasts
1 cup	(*250 mL*) peach slices (if using canned, drain well)
6 oz	(*170 g*) Brie cheese
2 tbsp	(*30 mL*) melted butter
1 cup	(*250 mL*) raspberry coulis (see *Sauces*)
½ cup	(*125 mL*) heavy cream

Preheat oven 350°F (*180°C*).

Pound each breast flat. Top with peach slices and cheese. Roll to fill the breast.

Place on a greased sheet and brush with butter. Place in oven and bake 15 minutes.

Pour raspberry coulis in saucepan, add cream and simmer 5 minutes.

Pour sauce over chicken and serve.

Chicken Melba

Chicken Cordon Bleu

6 servings

6	boneless chicken breasts, 6 oz (*170 g*) each
6 oz	(*170 g*) Black Forest ham
6 oz	(*170 g*) Swiss cheese
2	eggs
¼ cup	(*60 mL*) milk
¼ cup	(*60 mL*) flour
2 cups	(*500 mL*) fine breadcrumbs
½ cup	(*125 mL*) oil
1 cup	(*250 mL*) Mornay Sauce (see *Sauces*)

Preheat oven to 350°F (*180°C*).

Pound the chicken breasts flat. Cut the ham and cheese in six equal portions.

Place 1 piece each of ham and cheese on a chicken breast.

Fold the breast to encase the ham and cheese.

Mix eggs with milk.

Dust each breast with flour. Dip in egg mixture. Roll in breadcrumbs.

Heat oil and shallow fry.

Bake in oven for 8 to 10 minutes.

Serve with Mornay sauce on the side.

Ginger Garlic Chicken Wings

Ginger Garlic Chicken Wings

4 servings

¼ cup	(*60 mL*) soya sauce
2 tsp	(*10 mL*) ground ginger
3 tbsp	(*45 mL*) brown sugar
1 tsp	(*5 mL*) garlic powder
2¼ lbs	(*1 kg*) chicken wings

Preheat oven to 350°F (*180°C*).

Mix the soya sauce, ginger, sugar and garlic powder together.

Pour over chicken wings and marinate for 2 hours.

Bake in oven for 1 hour.

Moo Goo Gai Pan

4 servings

2 tbsp	(30 mL)	soya sauce
2 tbsp	(30 mL)	white wine
½ tsp	(3 mL)	salt
½ tsp	(3 mL)	sugar
2 tsp	(10 mL)	oil
1 tsp	(5 mL)	vinegar
1 lb	(450 g)	diced chicken
¼ cup	(60 mL)	oil
1 cup	(250 mL)	Chinese cabbage
4 oz	(115 g)	mushrooms, sliced
1		green pepper, diced
1		carrot, sliced
8 oz	(225 g)	bamboo shoots
¼ cup	(60 mL)	sliced water chestnuts

Mix the soya sauce, wine, salt, sugar, 2 tsp (10 mL) oil and vinegar together.

Pour over chicken and marinate for 1 hour.

Heat ¼ cup (60 mL) oil in a wok or large frying pan.

Discard the marinade and brown the chicken.

Add vegetables and cook for 3 minutes.

Serve with a rice pilaf.

Chicken à la King

6 servings

½ lb	(225 g)	button mushrooms
¼ cup	(60 mL)	diced green peppers
1		small onion, diced
2		celery stalks, sliced
¼ cup	(60 mL)	butter
¼ cup	(60 mL)	flour
2 cups	(500 mL)	heavy cream
1½ lbs	(675 g)	chicken, cooked and diced
3		egg yolks
½ tsp	(3 mL)	paprika
¼ cup	(60 mL)	sherry
¼ cup	(60 mL)	diced pimiento
		salt and pepper to taste

Sauté the mushrooms, peppers, onion and celery in the butter until tender.

Add flour and blend well. Add cream, chicken and simmer until slightly thickened.

Whip together the egg yolks, paprika, sherry and pimiento. Fold into sauce. Simmer for 5 minutes.

Season to taste and serve in vol-au-vent shells or over toast.

Chicken Newburg

4 servings

¼ cup	(60 mL)	butter
2 oz	(60 g)	mushrooms, sliced
2 tbsp	(30 mL)	minced onion
1 lb	(450 g)	chicken, cooked and diced
¼ cup	(60 mL)	sherry
1 cup	(250 mL)	light cream
½ tsp	(3 mL)	salt
½ tsp	(3 mL)	paprika
pinch		white pepper
3		egg yolks
8 cups	(2 L)	water
2 cups	(500 mL)	raw rice

In a saucepan, heat the butter and sauté the mushrooms and onion until tender.

Add the chicken and the sherry. Simmer for 5 minutes.

Add the cream and the seasonings and simmer 5 more minutes.

Remove a little of the hot sauce and mix with the egg yolk.

Return this mixture to the chicken and simmer until sauce has thickened.

In another pan, heat the water. Add the rice and stir 2 minutes. Once rice has cooked, drain.

Place rice in a serving dish. Pour Chicken Newburg over rice and serve.

Pamela's Favorite Chicken and Rice

8-10 servings

1 lb	(*450 g*) boneless chicken, diced
1 lb	(*450 g*) sliced tender veal, pounded very thin, in julienne strips
¼ cup	(*60 mL*) butter
2	medium carrots, coarsely grated
2	celery stalks, finely chopped
4	green onions, thinly sliced
¼ cup	(*60 mL*) flour
2 cups	(*500 mL*) chicken stock
2 cups	(*500 mL*) heavy cream
3 cups	(*750 mL*) cooked rice
1½ cups	(*375 mL*) coarsely grated Swiss cheese
1½ cups	(*375 mL*) coarsely grated medium Cheddar cheese

Preheat oven to 450°F (*230°C*).

In a heavy skillet, sauté the chicken and veal in butter over medium heat until cooked through. Stir in the vegetables, and sauté just until tender, about 2 to 3 minutes. Add the flour, chicken stock and cream. Simmer until thickened. Spread the rice in a greased 13 x 9 in. (*33 x 23 cm*) baking dish; pour the chicken mixture over it, and sprinkle with the grated cheeses.

Bake in oven 6 to 8 minutes or just until the cheese melts.

1

In a skillet, sauté the chicken and veal in butter over medium heat until cooked through.

2

Add the flour, chicken stock and cream; simmer until thickened.

3

Spread the rice in a greased baking dish and pour chicken mixture over it.

4

Sprinkle with grated cheeses and bake in oven 6 to 8 minutes, or until cheese melts.

Sautéed Pheasant with Clementine Sauce

6 servings

3 tbsp	(*45 mL*) oil
6	pheasant breasts, 6 oz (*170 g*) each
	salt and pepper to taste
⅓ cup	(*80 mL*) tangerine concentrate
½ cup	(*125 mL*) chicken stock
¼ cup	(*60 mL*) heavy cream
2 tbsp	(*30 mL*) butter
1 tsp	(*5 mL*) lime juice
	fresh cracked black pepper

Heat the oil in a large skillet.

Sauté the pheasant 4 to 6 minutes each side. Season with salt and pepper. Keep warm.

In a saucepan, add the tangerine concentrate and chicken stock. Bring to a boil and reduce heat.

Add cream and simmer 6 minutes or until sauce coats a spoon.

Whisk in the butter and lime juice. Add just a touch of pepper. Pour sauce over pheasant breasts and serve.

Sautéed Pheasant with Clementine Sauce

Pheasant Casserole

4 servings

½ cup	(*125 mL*) butter
2	onions, thinly sliced
4	carrots, pared and julienned
2	pheasants, 2¼ lbs (*1 kg*) each, cut into 4 pieces each
2 tbsp	(*30 mL*) flour
1 cup	(*250 mL*) red wine
½ cup	(*125 mL*) sherry
¼ cup	(*60 mL*) brandy
½ cup	(*125 mL*) chicken stock
	salt and pepper
¼ lb	(*115 g*) bacon, diced
12	pearl onions
20	button mushrooms

Preheat oven to 325°F (*160°C*).

In a large pot, heat half the butter and sauté the sliced onions and carrots until tender.

Add the pheasant and brown. Sprinkle in the flour and stir until the flour has absorbed the butter. Pour in the wine, sherry, brandy, stock and sprinkle with salt and pepper. Bring to a boil. Reduce heat and simmer 20 minutes.

In a saucepan, sauté the bacon, pearl onions and mushrooms until brown.

Place pheasant in a casserole dish. Spoon on the onions, bacon and mushrooms. Pour over the sauce. Cover.

Bake in oven for 60 minutes.

Thanksgiving Turkey

8-10 servings

Stuffing

½ cup	(*125 mL*) diced celery
1	large onion, diced
2	small carrots, diced
1 cup	(*250 mL*) butter
1 tsp	(*5 mL*) sage
1 tsp	(*5 mL*) basil
1 tsp	(*5 mL*) oregano
1 tsp	(*5 mL*) thyme
1 tsp	(*5 mL*) black pepper
2 tsp	(*10 mL*) salt
2¼ lbs	(*1 kg*) breadcrumbs
1 cup	(*250 mL*) raisins
2	eggs
½ cup	(*125*) cashews (optional)

Preheat oven to 375°F (*190°C*).

Sauté the celery, onion and carrots in the butter until tender. Add seasonings and sauté 1 minute. Pour mixture into a bowl; add breadcrumbs, raisins, eggs and cashews. Mix thoroughly. Stuff into a 12-14 lb (*5,4-6,3 kg*) turkey.

Turkey

12-14 lb (*5,4-6,3 kg*) turkey
½	lemon
1	garlic clove
2 tsp	(*10 mL*) salt

Rub turkey with garlic and lemon. Sprinkle with salt. Roast 4-5 hours, basting often.

Roast Duckling Grand Marnier

4 servings

1	duck, cut into 8 pieces
	salt and pepper
¼ cup	(*60 mL*) oil
2 cups	(*500 mL*) orange juice
¼ cup	(*60 mL*) Grand Marnier liqueur
1 cup	(*250 mL*) apricots, pitted and chopped
1 cup	(*250 mL*) plums, pitted and chopped
2 tbsp	(*30 mL*) flour
2 tbsp	(*30 mL*) water
4 cups	(*1 L*) cooked rice, hot

Remove the fat and trim the meat of the duck. Season with salt and pepper.

Brown in the oil. Add the orange juice and Grand Marnier and simmer until meat is tender.

Add the apricots and plums and simmer an additional 45 minutes.

Mix the flour with the water into a paste.

Add to the sauce and simmer until thickened.

Pour over rice and serve.

Roast Duck Bigarade

4 servings

4½ lb	(*2 kg*) duck
1 tbsp	(*15 mL*) butter
	salt and pepper
¾ cup	(*180 mL*) white wine
1	lemon
1	orange
1 tbsp	(*15 mL*) sugar
1 tbsp	(*15 mL*) sherry
1 cup	(*250 mL*) orange juice
2 tbsp	(*30 mL*) brandy
1 tbsp	(*15 mL*) cornstarch

Preheat oven to 375°F (*190°C*).

Rub the duck with the butter and season with salt and pepper. Place in a roasting pan and add the wine. Place in oven and roast for 2 to 2½ hours. Baste every 15 to 20 minutes with the wine.

Grate the lemon and orange rinds into a sauté pan. Melt the sugar in the pan with the sherry and cook until caramel in color, being careful not to let it burn.

Add the orange juice, the juice of the lemon and brandy. Simmer for 5 minutes. Cut the orange into segments and add to the sauce.

Remove duck from oven when done. Carve and place on platter. Drain fat from roasting pan and add the sauce to the duck drippings.

Mix a little water with the cornstarch and add to sauce. Bring to a boil for 2 minutes.

Pour over duck and serve.

Preheat oven to 350°F (*180°C*).

Prick skin of duck all over with a fork. Place duck in a roasting pan, surround with vegetables, and add 3 cups (*750 mL*) water.

Roast, uncovered, in oven 25 minutes per pound (*450 g*), or until cooked through.

Meanwhile, bring Espagnole Sauce to a boil and reduce to 1¼ cups (*310 mL*).

Drain cherries, reserving ½ cup (*125 mL*) juice.

Combine reduced Espagnole Sauce, reserved cherry juice, sherry, orange rind, and orange juice.

Remove duck from roasting pan; keep warm.

Discard vegetables from pan juices and drain off all fat.

Stir 1 cup (*250 mL*) pan juices into Espagnole Sauce mixture.

Bring to a boil and reduce, stirring constantly, to about 1¼ cups (*310 mL*).

Add icing sugar, cinnamon and cream cheese; stir until smooth.

Stir in cherries. Carve duck and serve accompanied with sauce.

Roast Duck Bigarade

Roast Duckling Montmorency

4 servings

1	4-5 lb (*2-2,5 kg*) duck
1	medium onion, quartered
2	carrots, coarsely chopped
2	celery stalks, coarsely chopped
2½ cups	(*625 mL*) Espagnole Sauce (see *Sauces*)
14 oz	(*398 mL*) can sweet cherries
½ cup	(*125 mL*) Brights Cream Sherry
2 tsp	(*10 mL*) grated orange rind
¼ cup	(*60 mL*) orange juice
3 tbsp	(*45 mL*) icing sugar
pinch	cinnamon
1	(*250 g*) pkg. cream cheese, cut into cubes

Roast Stuffed Cornish Hens

Roast Stuffed Cornish Hens

6 servings

8 cups	*(2 L)*	chicken stock
2 cups	*(500 mL)*	wild rice
1 tsp	*(5 mL)*	salt
½ tsp	*(3 mL)*	pepper
½ cup	*(125 mL)*	butter
¼ tsp	*(1 mL)*	chervil
¼ tsp	*(1 mL)*	basil
1 tsp	*(5 mL)*	chives
1 tbsp	*(15 mL)*	chopped parsley
¼ cup	*(60 mL)*	minced celery
2 tbsp	*(30 mL)*	minced onion
6		Cornish game hens, 12 oz *(340 g)* each
2 tsp	*(10 mL)*	paprika

Pour chicken stock into large pot or Dutch oven. Add wild rice, salt and pepper.

Bring to a boil, reduce heat, cover and simmer for 45 to 50 minutes.

Preheat oven to 350°F *(180°C)*.

Drain and stir the rice.

Blend in ¼ cup *(60 mL)* butter, chervil, basil, chives, chopped parsley, celery and onion. Stuff into cavity of hens and tie hens with string. Place hens in a roasting pan.

Melt the remaining butter. Brush the hens with butter. Sprinkle with paprika.

Bake in oven for 45 to 60 minutes or until hens are tender. Serve.

Chicken Curry

4 servings

2 tbsp	*(30 mL)*	butter
2		garlic cloves, minced
1½ cups	*(375 mL)*	chopped apples
½ cup	*(125 mL)*	chopped onions
1 tsp	*(5 mL)*	salt
1 tbsp	*(15 mL)*	curry powder
2 tbsp	*(30 mL)*	flour
2 cups	*(500 mL)*	light cream
2 cups	*(500 mL)*	cooked, diced chicken

In a saucepan, melt butter and add garlic, apples and onions. Sauté until tender.

Add salt, curry powder and flour. Blend well.

Gradually add cream, chicken and simmer 5 minutes. Serve over rice.

Chicken Divan

4 servings

4 cups	(*1 L*) broccoli florets
2 cups	(*500 mL*) Golden Mashed Potatoes
1 lb	(*450 g*) cooked boneless chicken breasts, diced
1⅓ cups	(*330 mL*) Mornay Sauce (see *Sauces*)
3	slices toast, cut into quarters diagonally

Preheat oven to 300°F (*150°C*).

Blanch broccoli florets just until tender crisp.

In a greased shallow baking dish, spread potatoes evenly.

Sprinkle with broccoli and diced chicken.

Drizzle with Mornay sauce and bake, uncovered, in oven 25 to 30 minutes or until heated through.

Place toast around rim of baking dish with points up.

Creamed Mace Chicken

6 servings

¼ cup	(*60 mL*) butter
¼ cup	(*60 mL*) flour
1 cup	(*250 mL*) chicken broth
2 cups	(*500 mL*) light cream
1 tsp	(*5 mL*) salt
¼ tsp	(*1 mL*) mace
¼ tsp	(*1 mL*) pepper
4 cups	(*1 L*) cooked boneless chicken, diced
8 cups	(*2 L*) cooked rice, hot

In a saucepan, heat the butter.

Add the flour and cook 2 minutes, while stirring.

Add the broth, cream and seasonings. Simmer until thickened, 10 to 12 minutes.

Stir in the chicken and simmer an additional 5 minutes.

Pour over rice and serve.

Rock Cornish Game Hens with Prune Stuffing

4 servings

Stuffing

2 cups	(*500 mL*) chicken stock
¼ cup	(*60 mL*) butter
1 cup	(*250 mL*) raw long-grain rice
1 tsp	(*5 mL*) salt
1 cup	(*250 mL*) finely chopped prunes
½ cup	(*125 mL*) walnuts

Rock Cornish Hens

4	rock Cornish game hens, 1 lb (*450 g*) each
¼ cup	(*60 mL*) melted butter
1 tbsp	(*15 mL*) salt

Preheat oven to 400°F (*200°C*).

In a saucepan, heat the chicken stock and melt the butter. Add the rice and salt and stir for 2 minutes. Cover and simmer 18 to 20 minutes.

Once cooked, rinse rice in a strainer under cold water. Mix the rice with the prunes and walnuts.

Carefully stuff the cavities of the birds with the stuffing. Brush each bird with the melted butter then season with salt.

Roast 35 to 50 minutes, basting with drippings every 10 to 15 minutes. Serve at once.

Pork

The great French chef Escoffier apparently thought pork was unworthy of classic cuisine, although he held ham in high regard.

Fortunately, today's chefs realize that pork, both fresh and cured, can play an important role in menu planning. In fact, pork is the second most popular red meat, next to beef.

Fresh pork is usually from young animals, and therefore tender. And although some people consider pork to be a fatty meat, certain cuts, including lean roasts and tenderloin, are lean enough to be adopted even in the most calorie-conscious diets.

Pork, unlike beef, should always be fresh, never aged. And it should always be cooked until well done, in order to eliminate the possibility of trichinosis.

Pork roasts should be cooked for 30 minutes per lb (*450 g*) at 325°F (*160°C*). It's a safe practice to use a meat thermometer, which should read 170°F (*76°C*) when the meat is properly cooked.

Hams are available fresh, cured or partly cured. Some of the most famous hams are Parma (prosciutto), Virginia (cured up to 2 years), Danish and York.

In this chapter you will find a number of pork recipes for fresh pork, including steaks, cutlets and roasts.

Pork Dijonnaise

Pork Dijonnaise

6 servings

6	pork shoulder chops
2 tbsp	(*30 mL*) butter
1 tsp	(*5 mL*) oil
2	green onions, diced
2	garlic cloves, minced
12	gherkins, julienned
½ cup	(*125 mL*) sherry
½ cup	(*125 mL*) heavy cream
2 tbsp	(*30 mL*) Dijon mustard

Sauté the pork chops in half the butter and oil, about 8-10 minutes each side.

In a saucepan, heat the rest of the butter. Sauté the onions and garlic until tender.

Add the gherkins and sherry. Simmer until most of liquid has evaporated.

Mix the mustard with the cream. Add to sauce; simmer 2 minutes.

Pour over pork chops and serve.

Pork Chops Baked in Mushroom Cream

8 servings

8	pork chops, 1-in. (2,5 cm) thick
2 tbsp	(30 mL) oil
4 oz	(115 g) mushrooms, sliced
2 tbsp	(30 mL) flour
1 cup	(250 mL) heavy cream
¼ cup	(60 mL) sherry
2 tsp	(10 mL) paprika
1 tsp	(5 mL) salt
½ tsp	(3 mL) black pepper

Preheat oven to 375°F (190°C).

Trim the chops of excess fat. Sauté the chops in a skillet in the oil, browning each side.

Transfer chops to a large casserole.

Place the mushrooms in the skillet and sauté until tender.

Sprinkle with flour and cook 2 minutes. Add the cream, sherry and seasonings.

Stir and gently simmer for 5 minutes. Pour sauce over chops.

Bake in oven for 30 minutes.

Serve with rice pilaf.

Breaded Pork Chops with Raisin Sauce

4 servings

1	egg
¼ cup	(60 mL) milk
8	pork chops
⅓ cup	(80 mL) flour
2 cups	(500 mL) breadcrumbs
¼ cup	(60 mL) oil

Sauce

1½ tbsp	(22 mL) cornstarch
½ cup	(125 mL) water
3 tbsp	(45 mL) brown sugar
1¼ cups	(310 mL) orange juice
2 tbsp	(30 mL) lemon juice
½ tsp	(3 mL) cinnamon
pinch	allspice
½ cup	(125 mL) raisins

Mix the egg in the milk. Dip the chops into the flour, then into the egg. Dredge in the breadcrumbs.

Heat the oil in a skillet. Fry the chops in the oil.

Sauce : Blend the cornstarch in the water. Dissolve the sugar in the orange juice.

Heat the orange juice in a saucepan.

Add the lemon juice and seasonings. Add the raisins and simmer for 5 minutes. Blend in the water and simmer until thick. Pour sauce over the chops and serve.

Orange Thyme Pork Chops

6 servings

6	pork shoulder chops
1 tsp	(5 mL) thyme
½ tsp	(3 mL) grated orange rind
1 cup	(250 mL) orange juice
2 tbsp	(30 mL) oil
pinch	salt and pepper

Trim the excess fat from the pork chops.

Mix the thyme, orange rind and orange juice together and pour over pork chops.

Marinate for 1 hour at room temperature.

Preheat oven to 375°F (190°C).

Remove pork chops and reserve marinade.

In a skillet, heat the oil and brown the chops. Place in a baking pan.

Pour marinade over chops, season and bake, covered, for 20 minutes.

Uncover and bake for another 5 minutes.

Stuffed Pork Chops

4 servings

¼ cup	*(60 mL)* minced onions
2 tbsp	*(30 mL)* minced celery
1 cup	*(250 mL)* breadcrumbs
½ cup	*(125 mL)* raisins
¼ cup	*(60 mL)* walnut pieces
½ tsp	*(3 mL)* thyme
½ tsp	*(3 mL)* basil
1 tbsp	*(15 mL)* chopped parsley
1 tsp	*(5 mL)* salt
⅓ cup	*(80 mL)* heavy cream
4	double rib pork chops
2 tbsp	*(30 mL)* oil
2 cups	*(500 mL)* Mornay Sauce (see *Sauces*)

Preheat oven to 350°F *(180°C)*.

In a mixing bowl, blend together onions, celery, breadcrumbs, raisins, walnuts and seasonings. Blend in the cream and mix thoroughly.

Trim the chops of any excess fat. Slice between the bones, creating a pocket. Stuff the filling into the pockets.

Heat the oil in a skillet. Brown the chops in the oil. Transfer to a casserole dish.

Cover the chops with the Mornay Sauce.

Cover and bake in oven for 45 minutes. Remove cover and degrease.

Place chops on platter. Smother with sauce.

1

In a mixing bowl, blend together onions, celery, breadcrumbs, raisins, walnuts and seasonings. Blend in the cream and mix thoroughly.

2

Trim the pork chops of fat and slice between the bones to create a pocket.

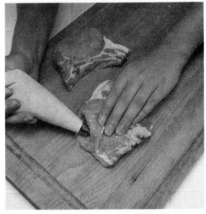

3

Stuff the filling into the pockets.

4

Pour Mornay Sauce over browned chops, cover and bake in oven for 45 minutes. Remove cover and degrease.

Roast Loin of Pork Provençale

8 servings

¼ cup	(60 mL) oil
7 lb	(3 kg) boneless pork loin, tied
¼ cup	(60 mL) minced onions
¼ cup	(60 mL) celery stalks, minced
¼ cup	(60 mL) green peppers, minced
3	garlic cloves, minced
1 cup	(250 mL) water
1 cup	(250 mL) red wine
2 cups	(500 mL) chopped tomatoes
2 tbsp	(30 mL) chopped parsley
½ tsp	(3 mL) thyme
1 tsp	(5 mL) salt
½ tsp	(3 mL) black pepper

Preheat oven to 350°F (180°C).

Heat the oil in a roasting pan. Brown the roast in the oil.

Add the onion, celery, green peppers and garlic. Pour the water and wine over the roast.

Add the tomatoes and seasonings. Cover and roast in oven 2½ hours. Remove roast, and keep warm.

Reduce sauce by simmering gently. Degrease.

Slice roast and serve with sauce.

Pork Steak with Mushroom Sauce

Pork Steak with Mushroom Sauce

8 servings

8	slices bacon
8	very lean pork steaks, 6 oz (170 g) each
¼ cup	(60 mL) butter
2 tbsp	(30 mL) minced onion
3 tbsp	(45 mL) diced green pepper
4 oz	(115 g) mushrooms
3 tbsp	(45 mL) flour
2 cups	(500 mL) demi-glace (see *Sauces*)
¼ cup	(60 mL) sherry
½ cup	(125 mL) heavy cream
¼ cup	(60 mL) diced green onions

Wrap the bacon around the steaks. Broil steaks over a charbroiler or in the oven until well done. Heat the butter in a skillet. Add the vegetables and sauté until tender. Sprinkle in flour. Cook for 2 minutes. Add the demi-glace and sherry and simmer for 5 minutes. Add the cream. Simmer 1 minute, add the green onions and simmer for 3 minutes.

Pour sauce over steaks. Serve at once.

Pork Schnitzel Milanese

Fry the cutlets in the oil, 2½ minutes each side. Remove and place on a pastry sheet.

Spoon 2 tbsp (*30 mL*) of sauce onto each cutlet. Sprinkle with cheese. Top with green peppers and mushrooms.

Broil in the oven 3 to 5 minutes until golden brown. Serve hot.

Pork Steak with Pepper Apple Sauce

4 servings

4	small pork steaks
2 tbsp	(*30 mL*) crushed black peppercorns
2 tbsp	(*30 mL*) flour
1 tbsp	(*15 mL*) brown sugar
2 tbsp	(*30 mL*) butter
2 tsp	(*10 mL*) green peppercorns
½ tsp	(*3 mL*) crushed white peppercorns
pinch	salt
2 tbsp	(*30 mL*) sherry
3 tbsp	(*45 mL*) applesauce

Pat the steaks in the crushed black peppercorns. Mix 1 tbsp (*15 mL*) flour with the sugar. Roll steaks in the sugared flour. Heat the butter and sauté the steaks. Remove and keep warm.

Add 1 tbsp (*15 mL*) flour to pan. Stir until browned.

Add the green peppercorns, white peppercorns, salt, sherry and applesauce. Simmer until thickened.

Pour over pork steaks and serve.

Pork Schnitzel Milanese

6 servings

6	pork cutlets, 4 oz (*115 g*) each
1	egg
¼ cup	(*60 mL*) milk
½ cup	(*125 mL*) flour
2 cups	(*500 mL*) seasoned breadcrumbs
¼ cup	(*60 mL*) olive oil
1½ cups	(*375 mL*) tomato sauce
2 cups	(*500 mL*) grated mozzarella cheese
½ cup	(*125 mL*) sliced green peppers
½ cup	(*125 mL*) sliced mushrooms

Pound the cutlets very thin. Blend egg with the milk. Dust the cutlets in the flour, dip into the egg and dredge in breadcrumbs.

Heat the oil in a large skillet.

Pork Tenderloin in Sour Cream Sauce

8 servings

¼ cup	(60 mL) oil
3 lbs	(1,4 kg) pork tenderloin, cubed
2 tbsp	(30 mL) butter
¼ cup	(60 mL) minced onions
4 oz	(115 g) mushrooms, sliced
1	garlic clove, minced
3 tbsp	(45 mL) flour
1 cup	(250 mL) chicken broth
1 cup	(250 mL) sour cream
1 tsp	(5 mL) paprika
½ tsp	(3 mL) cracked pepper
1 tsp	(5 mL) salt

Heat the oil in a large skillet. Sauté the tenderloin to brown. Remove and keep warm.

Add the butter to the skillet.

Sauté the onions, mushrooms and garlic until tender. Sprinkle with the flour. Cook for 2 minutes.

Add the broth, sour cream and seasonings. Simmer for 5 minutes.

Return the pork to skillet. Gently simmer for 10 minutes.

Serve with hot buttered noodles.

Pork Tenderloin Stroganoff

8 servings

¼ cup	(60 mL) butter
1	onion, thinly sliced
4 oz	(115 g) mushrooms, sliced
2¼ lbs	(1 kg) pork tenderloin, diced
2 tbsp	(30 mL) flour
1 cup	(250 mL) beef broth
½ cup	(125 mL) white wine
1 cup	(250 mL) sour cream
2 tsp	(10 mL) salt
½ tsp	(3 mL) cracked pepper
2 tsp	(10 mL) paprika
1 tbsp	(15 mL) prepared mustard

Heat the butter in a large skillet.

Add the onion and mushrooms. Sauté until tender.

Add the pork and brown. Sprinkle with flour. Cook 2 minutes.

Add the broth, wine and sour cream. Stir and simmer for 5 minutes.

Add seasonings and mustard. Simmer 30 more minutes.

Serve over noodles or rice.

Pork Tenderloin Diane

6 servings

¼ cup	(60 mL) butter
2¼ lbs	(1 kg) pork tenderloin, cubed
4 oz	(115 g) mushrooms, sliced
6	green onions, diced
¼ cup	(60 mL) brandy
¼ cup	(60 mL) sherry
2 cups	(500 mL) demi-glace (see *Sauces*)
½ cup	(125 mL) heavy cream

In a skillet, heat the butter. Sauté the tenderloin in the butter. Remove and keep warm.

Add the mushrooms and onions to the butter and cook until tender.

Add the brandy and flame carefully. Add the sherry and demi-glace. Simmer gently for 5 minutes. Finish by swirling in the cream.

Return the pork to skillet and simmer for an additional 3 minutes.

Serve at once.

Pork Tenderloin Diane

Italian Pork Tenderloin

Italian Pork Tenderloin

8 servings

¼ cup	(60 mL) olive oil
2¼ lbs	(1 kg) pork tenderloin, cubed
1	garlic clove, minced
1	onion, finely diced
1	green pepper, finely diced
2	celery stalks, finely diced
½ lb	(225 g) button mushrooms
3 cups	(750 mL) tomatoes, seeded and chopped
1 tsp	(5 mL) thyme
1 tsp	(5 mL) salt
½ tsp	(3 mL) cracked pepper
½ tsp	(3 mL) oregano
½ tsp	(3 mL) basil
1 lb	(450 g) fettuccine

Heat the oil in a large skillet. Sauté the pork until browned. Remove and keep warm.

Add the garlic, onion, green pepper, celery and mushrooms; sauté until tender.

Stir in the tomatoes and seasonings. Simmer gently for 20 minutes.

Return the pork to skillet and simmer 5 to 7 minutes.

While the sauce is reducing, boil water in a large pot. Add salt and fettuccine. Cook al dente.

Place drained fettucine on a platter.

Serve pork mixture over noodles.

Cabbage Rolls

18 rolls — 6 servings

1	cabbage
2 tbsp	(*30 mL*) bacon drippings
1 cup	(*250 mL*) diced onion
2	garlic cloves, minced
1 lb	(*450 g*) lean ground pork
¾ cup	(*180 mL*) cooked rice
2	eggs, beaten
2 tbsp	(*30 mL*) paprika
¼ tsp	(*1 mL*) oregano
1 tsp	(*5 mL*) salt
1 tsp	(*5 mL*) pepper
1 lb	(*450 g*) sauerkraut
½ cup	(*125 mL*) chicken stock
½ cup	(*125 mL*) tomato purée
2 cups	(*500 mL*) sour cream

Preheat oven to 350°F (*180°C*).

Boil cabbage until leaves are tender enough to roll.

Heat the bacon drippings and brown the onion and garlic.

Mix the pork, browned onion and garlic, rice, eggs and seasonings together. Stuff into leaves and roll.

Place sauerkraut on the bottom of a casserole dish. Place rolls on top of sauerkraut.

Mix chicken stock with tomato purée.

Pour over rolls. Cover and bake in oven for 1¾ hours. Serve with sour cream.

1

Mix the ground pork, browned onion and garlic, rice, eggs and seasonings together.

2

Stuff mixture into cabbage leaves and roll.

3

Spread sauerkraut on the bottom of casserole dish and place cabbage rolls on top.

4

Mix chicken stock with tomato purée and pour over rolls.

Veal, Lamb and other Meats

North Americans have not been as adventurous as people in other parts of the world when it comes to meats.

Lamb, especially, is far more common on menus in other countries than it is here. However, more and more, our finest restaurants are featuring lamb dishes, and receiving an enthusiastic response. And these are not simply the old standbys of lamb chops or rack of lamb, but variations based on a whole gamut of cuts : steaks, crown roast, leg, loin roast, saddle roast and shoulder roast.

Cook lamb as you would beef. If you prefer your beef cooked rare or medium, chances are you'll like lamb done the same way.

Veal is a delicate meat that requires little cooking. "True" veal comes from calves no more that 14 weeks old, but in fact an acceptable product is obtained from animals up to a year old.

Because veal comes from young animals, it has not had the chance to develop much fat. The best veal is very pale pink, but is darker from older animals.

Veal is a relatively expensive meat, so beware of cheap "veal cutlets" in second-class restaurants. It's quite likely that pork has been substituted for the veal.

Game meats are becoming increasingly popular and available in North America. They can make a wonderful change from more common meats, and are not really complicated to prepare. Consider one of the game recipes in this chapter on those occasions when you want to surprise your guests with something really different.

Veal Medallions with Oyster Mushrooms and Brandy Sauce

Veal Medallions with Oyster Mushrooms and Brandy Sauce

6 servings

2 lbs	(*900 g*) veal tenderloin
¼ cup	(*60 mL*) butter
1 lb	(*450 g*) oyster mushrooms
3 tbsp	(*45 mL*) brandy
3 tbsp	(*45 mL*) sherry
2 cups	(*500 mL*) demi-glace (see *Sauces*)
½ cup	(*125 mL*) heavy cream

Cut the tenderloin into medallions.

Sauté the medallions in the butter, 2 minutes each side.

Remove the medallions and keep warm in oven.

Add the mushrooms to the butter and sauté until tender. Flame with the brandy.

Stir in the sherry and demi-glace. Simmer for 3 minutes and add cream. Simmer 3 more minutes.

Pour sauce over medallions and serve.

Veal Medallions in Shrimp Sauce

4 servings

2 tbsp	(*30 mL*) oil
2 tbsp	(*30 mL*) butter
8	veal medallions, 3 oz (*90 g*) each
3 tbsp	(*45 mL*) flour
¾ cup	(*180 mL*) veal or chicken stock (see *Soups*)
½ cup	(*125 mL*) heavy cream
¼ cup	(*60 mL*) sherry
½ tsp	(*3 mL*) salt
¼ tsp	(*1 mL*) pepper
¾ cup	(*180 mL*) baby shrimp

Heat the oil and butter in a skillet.

Sauté the veal in the butter 3½ minutes each side. Transfer to a heat-proof plate. Keep warm in oven.

Sprinkle the flour into the skillet; cook for 2 minutes.

Add the stock, cream, sherry and seasonings. Simmer for 2 minutes over low heat.

Add the shrimp and simmer 2 more minutes.

Pour sauce over veal. Serve at once.

Veal Piccata

4 servings

4	veal escalopes, 6 oz (*170 g*) each
2 tbsp	(*30 mL*) flour
¼ cup	(*60 mL*) butter
1	garlic clove, minced
¼ cup	(*60 mL*) dry sherry
1 tbsp	(*15 mL*) lemon juice
½	lemon, sliced

Place the veal between 2 pieces of wax paper. Pound very thin.

Dust the veal with flour.

Melt the butter and sauté the garlic. Remove the garlic bits and sauté the veal 2 ½ minutes each side.

Remove and keep warm.

Pour the sherry and lemon juice in the pan; simmer 3 minutes.

Pour sauce over veal.

Garnish with lemon slices and serve.

Escalope of Veal Cordon Bleu

8 servings

8	veal escalopes, pounded to a thickness of ⅛ in. (*0,5 cm*), about 3 oz (*90 g*) each
8 oz	(*250 g*) thinly sliced Black Forest ham
8	slices Swiss cheese
½ cup	(*125 mL*) all-purpose flour
3	eggs, well-beaten
2 tbsp	(*30 mL*) milk
2 cups	(*500 mL*) fine dry breadcrumbs
½ tsp	(*3 mL*) salt
½ tsp	(*3 mL*) pepper
	oil for frying
	Mushroom and Parmesan Cream Sauce (see *Sauces*)

Preheat oven to 400°F (*200°C*).

On one side of each veal escalope, place 1 oz (*30 g*) ham and 1 slice of cheese. Fold the other side over and pinch edges to seal.

Dip each escalope in flour, then into a mixture of eggs and milk, and then into breadcrumbs seasoned with salt and pepper.

Fry in ½ in. (*1 cm*) hot oil until browned, about 3 minutes each side.

Bake 12 minutes in oven to make outside crisp.

Serve with Mushroom and Parmesan Cream Sauce.

Veal Scaloppine Velez

8 servings

8	veal escalopes
½ cup	(*125 mL*) all-purpose flour
2	eggs, beaten
¾ cup	(*180 mL*) fine dry breadcrumbs
1 tsp	(*5 mL*) salt
pinch	pepper
pinch	rubbed thyme
pinch	dried basil leaves
⅓ cup	(*80 mL*) butter
¼ cup	(*60 mL*) vegetable oil
1 lb	(*450 g*) thinly sliced ham
16	cooked asparagus spears
2 cups	(*500 mL*) coarsely grated Havarti cheese

Dip each veal escalope first into flour, then into the beaten eggs, and then into a mixture of breadcrumbs, salt, pepper, thyme and basil.

Heat butter and oil in a large skillet. Sauté the escalopes over high heat, about 2 ½ minutes each side.

Top each escalope with 2 oz (*60 g*) ham and 2 asparagus spears. Sprinkle with grated cheese and place under a heated broiler just until cheese melts.

Veal Scaloppine Velez

Veal John B. Hoyle

8 servings

8	veal escalopes about 5 oz (*150 g*) each pounded to a thickness of about ⅛ in. (*0,5 cm*)
½ lb	(*225 g*) cooked baby shrimp
2	Granny Smith apples, peeled and chooped
2 cups	(*500 mL*) grated Colby cheese
	salt and pepper
¼ cup	(*60 mL*) melted butter
1⅓ cups	(*330 mL*)Mornay Sauce (see *Sauces*)

Preheat oven to 350°F (*180°C*)

Top each veal escalope with shrimp, chopped apples and cheese. Roll tightly and place, seam side down, in a greased, shallow baking dish. Season and brush with butter.

Bake, covered, in oven 15 to 20 minutes or until veal is cooked through.

Transfer rolls to a serving plate and drizzle with Mornay Sauce.

Veal Meatballs

4 servings

2	slices bacon, finely chopped
1	onion, finely chopped
1 lb	(*450 g*) ground veal
¼ tsp	(*1 mL*) rubbed thyme
¼ tsp	(*1 mL*) dried oregano leaves
¼ tsp	(*1 mL*) dried basil leaves
¼ tsp	(*1 mL*) garlic powder
1 tsp	(*5 mL*) salt
1	egg
½ cup	(*125 mL*) fine dry breadcrumbs
1 cup	(*250 mL*) grated Parmesan cheese
2 tbsp	(*30 mL*) vegetable oil
½ cup	(*125 mL*) beef stock (see *Soups*)
½ cup	(*125 mL*) white wine
2 tbsp	(*30 mL*) minced parsley
	cooked pasta or rice, hot

Veal Meatballs

In a large skillet, sauté bacon until cooked but still tender; set aside. In the bacon fat, sauté onion until tender.

Combine bacon, onion, veal, seasonings, egg, breadcrumbs, and cheese; blend well with your fingers. Shape into 1-in. (*2,5 cm*) meatballs.

Brown the meatballs in bacon fat, adding vegetable oil if necessary, until the sides of the meatballs are crisp; drain.

Add beef stock and wine; simmer meatballs, uncovered, 15 to 20 minutes until cooked through.

Spoon the meatballs over hot, cooked pasta or rice, drizzle with about half the stock, and sprinkle with parsley.

Veal Croquettes

6 servings

1 ½ lbs	(*675 g*) ground veal
2 tbsp	(*30 mL*) vegetable oil
3 tbsp	(*45 mL*) butter
3	mushrooms, finely chopped
3 tbsp	(*45 mL*) all-purpose flour
1 cup	(*250 mL*) heavy cream
½ cup	(*125 mL*) beef stock (see *Soups*)
1 tbsp	(*15 mL*) chopped fresh parsley
¼ tsp	(*1 mL*) nutmeg
¼ tsp	(*1 mL*) salt
¼ tsp	(*1 mL*) pepper

(Continued on next page)

6 oz	(*175 g*) Swiss cheese, in a block
¼ tsp	(*1 mL*) salt
¼ tsp	(*1 mL*) pepper
2 cups	(*500 mL*) fine dry breadcrumbs
¼ cup	(*60 mL*) all-purpose flour
2	eggs, well beaten
	oil for frying

Sauté the veal in oil and half the butter until no pink remains; drain and set aside.

Sauté the mushrooms in the remaining butter, stir in 3 tbsp (*45 mL*) flour. Add the cream, stock, parsley, nutmeg, salt and pepper; simmer stirring, until thickened.

Stir in the meat; cool completely.

Cut cheese into six sticks. Pat meat around each stick.

Add salt and pepper to breadcrumbs.

Roll each croquette in flour, then in eggs, and finally in seasoned breadcrumbs. Heat the oil to 375°F (*190°C*) and deep fry until golden.

Carré d'Agneau

Carré d'Agneau

1 serving

1	rack of lamb
2 tbsp	(*30 mL*) Dijon mustard
¼ cup	(*60 mL*) ground hazelnuts
2 tbsp	(*30 mL*) fine breadcrumbs
1 tbsp	(*15 mL*) Romano cheese
1 tbsp	(*15 mL*) melted butter

Have the butcher remove the backbone of the rack of lamb.

Preheat oven to 400°F (*200°C*).

Trim all the fat. Trim the meat from top and in between each rib bone. Crack the bones at the joints.

Spread the mustard over the meat.

Mix the hazelnuts, breadcrumbs and cheese together. Sprinkle over the mustard, covering completely.

Sprinkle with melted butter. Roast in oven for 30 minutes.

Serve with your choice of Béarnaise Sauce or mint jelly preserves.

Roast Lamb Rack

1 serving

1	rack of lamb
2 tbsp	(*30 mL*) olive oil
1 tsp	(*5 mL*) coarse salt
½ tsp	(*3 mL*) rosemary
½ tsp	(*3 mL*) cracked pepper
¼ tsp	(*1 mL*) oregano
¼ tsp	(*1 mL*) basil
¼ tsp	(*1 mL*) paprika

Have the butcher remove the backbone of the rack of lamb.

Preheat oven to 400°F (*200°C*).

Trim all the fat. Trim meat from top and in between each rib bone. Crack bones at the joint.

Rub meat with olive oil. Sprinkle with seasonings and salt.

Roast in oven for 30 minutes. Serve with Apple Mint Sauce.

Apple Mint Sauce (*per serving*)

1 tbsp	(*15 mL*) butter
2 tbsp	(*30 mL*) brown sugar
½ cup	(*125 mL*) apples, pared, cored and diced
1½ tsp	(*8 mL*) chopped fresh mint
¼ cup	(*60 mL*) apple juice

Heat the butter in a saucepan. Add the sugar and caramelize. Add the apples, mint and juice. Simmer 5 to 6 minutes. Serve on the side with rack of lamb.

Lamb Loaf

8 servings

2¼ lbs	(*1 kg*) lean ground lamb
½ cup	(*125 mL*) breadcrumbs
2	eggs
1 tsp	(*5 mL*) salt
½ tsp	(*3 mL*) pepper
1 tbsp	(*15 mL*) chopped chives
1 tbsp	(*15 mL*) chopped parsley
½ tsp	(*3 mL*) basil
1 tsp	(*5 mL*) grated lemon rind

Preheat oven to 350°F (*180°C*).

In a large mixing bowl, blend the lamb, breadcrumbs and eggs.

Add the seasonings and lemon rind. Combine thoroughly. Shape into a loaf. Bake in oven for 60 minutes.

New Zealand Roast Lamb

8 servings

5 lb	(*2,2 kg*) lamb shoulder, boned, rolled and tied
¼ cup	(*60 mL*) oil
2 tsp	(*10 mL*) salt
½ tsp	(*3 mL*) black pepper
2 cups	(*500 mL*) Honey-Mustard Sauce (see *Sauces*)

Preheat oven to 350°F (*180°C*).

Rub the lamb with the oil. Sprinkle with salt and pepper. Roast in oven for 1 ½ hours. During the final 15 minutes, brush with sauce every 5 minutes, then once more just before serving.

Serve remaining sauce with the roast.

Shish Kebab Flambé

6 servings

2 tsp	(*10 mL*) garlic powder
½ tsp	(*3 mL*) basil
½ tsp	(*3 mL*) oregano
2 tsp	(*10 mL*) salt
½ tsp	(*3 mL*) coriander
½ tsp	(*3 mL*) cumin
¼ tsp	(*1 mL*) turmeric
pinch	ginger
1 cup	(*250 mL*) sherry
⅓ cup	(*80 mL*) olive oil
1 tbsp	(*15 mL*) lemon juice
2¼ lbs	(*1 kg*) lamb, cut in 1½ in. (*4 cm*) cubes
⅓ cup	(*80 mL*) brandy

Blend all the seasonings together with the sherry, oil and lemon juice in a mixing bowl. Add the cubed lamb.

Marinate overnight or for 8 hours. Place meat on skewers. Leave small gaps between each piece. Broil 3 minutes each side, preferably on a charcoal broiler.

Place skewers on a platter when cooked. Pour brandy over. Ignite carefully. Serve while flaming.

Herb and Cheese Lamb Cutlets

6 servings

6	lamb cutlets, 4 oz (*115 g*) each
½ tsp	(*3 mL*) basil
½ tsp	(*3 mL*) marjoram
1 tsp	(*5 mL*) chopped chives
½ tsp	(*3 mL*) cracked pepper
12 oz	(*340 g*) cream cheese
1	egg
¼ cup	(*60 mL*) milk
⅓ cup	(*80 mL*) flour
2 cups	(*500 mL*) breadcrumbs
½ cup	(*125 mL*) oil
2 cups	(*500 mL*) Mornay Sauce (see *Sauces*)

Preheat oven to 350°F (*180°C*).

Pound the cutlets thin.

Blend the herbs and the pepper into the cheese.

Place 2 oz (*60 g*) of blended cheese on each cutlet. Wrap meat around the cheese.

Mix the egg in the milk. Dust cutlets with flour. Dip into milk. Dredge in breadcrumbs.

Heat oil in a skillet. Brown the cutlets in the oil.

Transfer to a baking sheet.

Bake 12 minutes in oven.

Heat Mornay Sauce. Serve sauce with cutlets.

1

Pound the lamb cutlets thin. Blend the herbs and the pepper into the cream cheese.

2

Place 2 oz (*60 g*) of blended cheese on each cutlet.

3

Wrap meat around the cheese.

4

Bake breaded cutlets 12 minutes in oven.

Buffalo Burgers

8 servings

2¼ lbs	(*1 kg*) ground buffalo meat
1 cup	(*250 mL*) breadcrumbs
2	eggs
1 tsp	(*5 mL*) salt
½ tsp	(*3 mL*) pepper
1 tbsp	(*15 mL*) Worcestershire sauce
1 tsp	(*5 mL*) basil
1 tsp	(*5 mL*) paprika

In a large mixing bowl, blend together the buffalo meat, breadcrumbs, eggs and seasonings. Shape into patties.

Broil over a charcoal broiler to desired doneness.

Buffalo Filets in Peppercorn Sauce

6 servings

6	buffalo filets, 6 oz (*170 g*) each
1 cup	(*250 mL*) demi-glace (see *Sauces*)
¼ cup	(*60 mL*) sherry
⅓ cup	(*80 mL*) heavy cream
¼ cup	(*60 mL*) red currant preserves
1 tbsp	(*15 mL*) green peppercorns

Broil the filets over a charcoal broiler to desired doneness.

Heat the demi-glace in a saucepan.

Add the sherry and reduce by half. Add the cream and the preserves and simmer for 3 minutes.

Add the peppercorns. Serve the sauce over the steaks.

Braised Buffalo Steak with Mushrooms

6 servings

2¼ lbs	(*1 kg*) buffalo round steak
1	egg, lightly beaten
3 tbsp	(*45 mL*) milk
2 cups	(*500 mL*) seasoned breadcrumbs
¼ cup	(*60 mL*) light oil
10 oz	(*284 g*) can mushrooms, with liquid
1 tbsp	(*15 mL*) flour

Cut steak to 1-in. (*2,5 cm*) thickness and serving size.

Dip into egg and milk mixture and then into the breadcrumbs.

Heat the oil in a large skillet. Brown the steaks 2 ½ minutes each side.

Pour mushrooms over the steaks with the liquid. Cover and simmer for 45 minutes.

Mix the flour with a little water; add to sauce a little at a time.

Simmer until thick. Serve at once.

Moose Roast

6-8 servings

1 lb	(*450 g*) salt pork (optional)
4 lb	(*1,8 kg*) rump moose roast
1 tbsp	(*15 mL*) dry mustard
2 tsp	(*10 mL*) salt
1 tsp	(*5 mL*) pepper
2	onions, sliced
2	carrots, chopped
2	celery stalks, chopped

2 cups	(*500 mL*) tomatoes, seeded, chopped and strained

Roll the salt pork out thin. Wrap the roast with the pork. Refrigerate overnight or 10 to 12 hours.*

Preheat oven to 300°F (*150°C*).

Remove and discard the pork. Rub thoroughly with dry mustard. Season with salt and pepper.

Place in a roasting pan. Surround with vegetables.

Pour tomatoes over vegetables.

Cover and bake in oven for 2 hours for medium doneness.

For well done, bake an additional 35 to 45 minutes.

* This adjusts the meat if it has a wild gamey odor which will affect the taste. This is dictated by the animals feeding ground and not age.

Moose Roast

Fish and Seafood

These days, people are eating more fish and shellfish than ever, and with good reason. Modern transportation makes good fresh fish available no matter where you live, and almost everyone likes at least some kind of fish — even many vegetarians!

And fish is a healthy choice, too. It's high in protein, low in calories and saturated fats.

In this chapter, you will find a variety of recipes for fish and shellfish, some of them almost sinfully rich and elegant, some of them incredibly simple, and all of them delicious.

Whatever recipes you try, remember that the most important thing is to start with perfectly fresh fish.

Plan to use fish the same day you buy it. If you must store it, keep it in the coldest part of the refrigerator. Shellfish keep best on ice.

How to Choose Fresh Fish

Fishermen will tell you the best fish they ever ate was the fish freshly-caught and put straight in the pan.

If you live near the seacoast, your best bet is to head to the markets where fishermen sell their catch fresh off the boat. But in the rest of the country, here are the signs of freshness you should look for:

1. Fresh fish has almost no smell. Never buy fish that has an objectionable odor or a particularly "fishy" smell.

2. The skin should be bright and shiny with the scales clinging closely. Eyes should be round and bright, not milky or sunken. The flesh inside the gills should be red or bright pink.

3. The flesh should feel firm to the touch, not soft.

Basic Cooking Tips

Whatever the species or cooking method, plan on cooking for 10 minutes per inch (2,5 cm) of thickness (measured at the thickest part of the fish or filet). If possible, choose to pan-fry, steam, bake or deep-fry fish. Fish cooked in water tends to dry out. If you want to poach your fish, be sure to use a fish fumet or court bouillon. (See the section on *Soups*).

Salmon Filets with Raspberry, Kiwi and Green Peppercorn Sauce

Salmon Filets with Raspberry, Kiwi and Green Peppercorn Sauce

4 servings

4	salmon filets
1 tbsp	(*15 mL*) melted butter
½ cup	(*125 mL*) heavy cream
1 cup	(*250 mL*) raspberries
¼ cup	(*60 mL*) sugar
1 tbsp	(*15 mL*) green peppercorns
2	kiwis

Preheat oven to 350°F (*180°C*).

Brush salmon with melted butter.

Bake in oven for 12 to 15 minutes.

In a saucepan, heat cream, raspberries, sugar and peppercorns. Simmer for 5 minutes.

Peel the kiwis and chop; add to sauce.

Remove salmon from oven.

Place filets on plates and pour sauce over salmon and serve.

Apples Stuffed with Smoked Salmon

6 servings

6	very large apples
1 lb	(450 g) fresh spinach
½ cup	(125 mL) butter
3 tbsp	(45 mL) all-purpose flour
1 tbsp	(15 mL) dried basil leaves
2½ cups	(625 mL) heavy cream
2	egg yolks
½ cup	(125 mL) grated Havarti cheese
1 lb	(450 g) smoked salmon

Preheat oven to 350°F (180°C).

Cut a ½-in. (1,5 cm) slice from the top of each apple. Hollow out the apple, leaving a ¼-in. (0,5 cm) shell all around. Take care not to pierce the apple skin.

Arrange the apple shells in a baking dish.

Quickly sauté the spinach in ¼ cup (60 mL) butter over high heat until wilted and tender. Chop and set aside.

Melt the remaining ¼ cup (60 mL) butter and stir in the flour. Add the basil and 2 cups (500 mL) cream; simmer until sauce has thickened.

Whisk the yolks into the remaining cream and stir into the sauce. Stir in the cheese and set aside.

Place half the salmon in the bottom of the apples. Spoon spinach over.

Place the remaining salmon on top. Fill with sauce.

Replace apple tops and bake in oven until apple skins are tender, 15 to 20 minutes.

Serve with rice pilaf and kernel corn mixed with pieces of sweet red pimiento.

Cheese scones are very nice with this as well.

Salmon with Crab and Béarnaise Sauce

4 servings

4 cups	(1 L) court bouillon (see *Soups*)
4	salmon filets, 6 oz (170 g) each
1 cup	(250 mL) crab meat, cooked
1 cup	(250 mL) Béarnaise Sauce (see *Sauces*)

Heat the court bouillon. Gently simmer the salmon in court bouillon 10 to 12 minutes.

Remove and place in a shallow pan. Top each filet with ¼ cup (60 mL) crab meat and 2 tbsp (30 mL) of Béarnaise Sauce.

Place under broiler for 1 minute or until brown.

Serve the remaining sauce on the side.

Baked Stuffed Salmon

8 servings

5 lb	(2,2 kg) fresh salmon
½ lb	(225 g) bacon, diced
1	onion, minced
1	celery stalk, minced
2	carrots, minced
2 cups	(500 mL) crackers, crushed fine
1 cup	(250 mL) lobster, shrimp or crab meat, cooked and chopped
1 tsp	(5 mL) paprika
¼ tsp	(1 mL) pepper
½ cup	(125 mL) water

Preheat oven to 375°F (190°C).

Thoroughly clean the salmon. Prepare stuffing by frying the bacon until tender.

Add the onion, celery and carrots. Sauté until tender. Drain excess fat. Cool.

Mix the crackers with the seafood and seasonings. Add the fried mixture.

Stuff into the cavity of the fish. Tie with string.

Bake in a greased covered baking pan 40 to 45 minutes with ½ cup (125 ml) water.

Poached Salmon with Blue Cheese Sauce

until fish flakes with a fork, about 8 to 12 minutes, depending on size of filets.

Serve hot or cold, accompanied with Blue Cheese Sauce.

Sauce : Combine all ingredients; mix well. Chill.

Salmon with Orange and Pecans

6 servings

3 tbsp	*(45 mL)* butter
6	salmon filets, 6 oz *(170 g)*
2 tbsp	*(30 mL)* flour
1 cup	*(250 mL)* heavy cream
¼ cup	*(60 mL)* sherry
1	orange
½ cup	*(125 mL)* chopped pecans

Preheat oven to 350°F (*180°C*).

Melt the butter in a saucepan. Use 1 tbsp (*15 mL*) of melted butter to brush on salmon. Bake salmon 12 to 15 minutes in oven.

Add the flour to the remaining butter. Stir and cook for 2 minutes.

Add the cream and sherry. Simmer until thickened.

Grate the orange peel and add to sauce. Stir in the pecans.

Remove fish from oven. Place on a serving platter. Smother with sauce.

Slice the orange and use as a garnish. Serve.

Poached Salmon with Blue Cheese Sauce

6 servings

6	salmon filets
	court bouillon (see *Soups*)

Blue Cheese Sauce

1 tbsp	*(15 mL)* pickle relish
2 tbsp	*(30 mL)* chopped parsley
2 tbsp	*(30 mL)* chopped chives
2 tbsp	*(30 mL)* heavy cream
2 tsp	*(10 mL)* lemon juice
1 tsp	*(5 mL)* Worcestershire sauce
¼ cup	*(60 mL)* crumbled blue cheese
1 cup	*(250 mL)* mayonnaise

Place the salmon filets in a large heavy skillet.

Cover with court bouillon. Bring to a boil over high heat; reduce heat and simmer just

Filet of Sole Olga

4 servings

4	large potatoes
4	sole filets 6 oz (*170 g*) each
4 cups	(*1 L*) court bouillon (see *Soups*)
1 cup	(*250 mL*) baby shrimp
1 cup	(*250 mL*) White Wine Sauce (see *Sauces*)
1 cup	(*250 mL*) grated Cheddar cheese

Preheat oven to 400°F (*200°C*).

Wash and scrub the potatoes.

Bake potatoes until tender in oven. Remove from oven.

Cut away the tops. Scoop out the pulp, leaving the shell.

Fold filets in half. Heat court bouillon. Gently poach the filets in the court bouillon.

Spoon 2 tbsp (*30 mL*) of shrimp into potatoes. Add the poached filets. Spoon in 2 tbsp (*30 mL*) of White Wine Sauce.

Sprinkle with cheese.

Return to over and bake 8 to 10 minutes or until cheese is golden brown. Serve.

Sole Meunière

4 servings

4	sole filets
⅓ cup	(*80 mL*) milk
½ cup	(*125 mL*) flour
⅓ cup	(*125*) butter
2 tbsp	(*30 mL*) freshly chopped parsley
1	lemon

Dip the filets in the milk. Dust the filets with the flour.

Heat the butter in a skillet. Sauté the filets in the butter 2½ to 3 minutes each side.

Remove filets to a heated platter.

Add the parsley and lemon juice to butter; cook for 1 minute.

Pour over filets and serve.

Sole Walewaska

4 servings

4 cups	(*1 L*) court bouillon (see *Soups*)
4	sole filets, 6 oz (*170 g*) each
1 cup	(*250 mL*) Mornay Sauce (see *Sauces*)
8 oz	(*225 g*) lobster meat
1 cup	(*250 mL*) grated Swiss cheese

Heat the court bouillon.

Gently poach the filets in the court bouillon 8 to 10 minutes.

Heat the Mornay Sauce in a saucepan.

Remove filets and place on an ovenproof platter.

Top each filet with 2 oz (*30 g*) of lobster meat. Cover with sauce. Sprinkle with cheese.

Broil in oven for 1 minute or until golden brown.

Filet of Sole Florentine

4 servings

4	sole filets, 8 oz (*225 g*) each
8 oz	(*225 g*) spinach leaves, chopped fine
6 cups	(*1,5 L*) court bouillon (see *Soups*)
½ cup	(*125 mL*) sherry
1½ cups	(*375 mL*) Mornay Sauce (see *Sauces*)

Top each filet with spinach, then roll each up like a jelly roll.

Hold together with toothpicks.

Bring court bouillon to a gentle boil and add the sherry.

Cook the fish in the court bouillon until opaque in color.

Place on serving platter. Keep hot.

Heat Mornay Sauce.

Pour sauce over fish and serve at once.

1
Top each sole filet with chopped spinach.

2
Roll each filet up like a jelly roll; hold together with toothpicks.

3
Boil the fish in the court bouillon and sherry until opaque in color.

4
Pour heated Mornay Sauce over fish and serve at once.

Filet of Sole with Mushrooms

4 servings

8 oz	(*225 g*) mushrooms, sliced
2 cups	(*500 mL*) water
1 cup	(*250 mL*) white wine
4	sole filets, 6 oz (*170 g*) each
3 tbsp	(*45 mL*) butter
3 tbsp	(*45 mL*) flour
1 cup	(*250 mL*) light cream
1 cup	(*250 mL*) Mornay Sauce (see *Sauces*)
¼ cup	(*60 mL*) fine breadcrumbs

Preheat oven to 500°F (*260°C*).

Boil the mushrooms in the water and wine for 7 minutes. Strain the mushrooms and reserve the liquid.

Poach fish in the mushroom liquid and keep hot in a casserole dish.

In a saucepan, melt the butter, add the flour and make a paste (roux).

Add the cream and mushrooms. Simmer until very thick. Mix in Mornay Sauce.

Pour this mixture over the fish.

Sprinkle with breadcrumbs.

Bake in oven until golden brown. Serve.

Filet of Sole Nantua

1 serving

1	sole filet, 8 oz (*225 g*)
6 cups	(*1,5 L*) court bouillon (see *Soups*)
2 tsp	(*10 mL*) butter
2 tsp	(*10 mL*) flour
3 tbsp	(*45 mL*) heavy cream
3 tbsp	(*45 mL*) fish stock (see *Soups*)
1 tbsp	(*15 mL*) chopped crayfish, or lobster meat
1 tbsp	(*15 mL*) shrimp, cooked and chopped
pinch	paprika
2 tsp	(*10 mL*) sherry

Gently poach the fish in the court bouillon.

Remove 1 cup (*250 mL*) of the court bouillon and simmer; reduce to 3 tbsp (*45 mL*).

In a saucepan, melt the butter and add the flour to make a paste (roux).

Add the cream and stock. Simmer 1 minute, add crayfish, shrimp, paprika and sherry.

Simmer 1 more minute.

Pour sauce over fish and serve.

Sole Normandy

4 servings

4	apples
1 cup	(*250 mL*) Béchamel Sauce (see *Sauces*)
1 cup	(*250 mL*) baby shrimp
½	sheet puff pastry
⅓ cup	(*80 mL*) butter
4 tsp	(*20 mL*) oil
4	sole filets, 7 oz (*200 g*) each
1 tsp	(*5 mL*) parsley
2 tsp	(*10 mL*) lemon juice

Preheat oven to 350°F (*180°C*).

Cut the tops from the apples. Scoop away the core and pulp, leaving a shell.

Mix the Béchamel Sauce with the shrimp. Stuff into the cavity of the apple. Bake in oven 20 to 25 minutes until the apples are tender.

Cut the puff pastry into 1 x 3-in. (*2,5 x 7,5 cm*) rectangles.

Bake in oven with the apples on a separate shelf.

In a skillet, melt 4 tsp (*20 mL*) butter together with the oil. Reduce heat.

Gently sauté the filets 2½ to 3 minutes each side. Remove fish to a heated serving platter.

Add the remaining butter, parsley and lemon juice.

Cook to very hot. Pour over fish.

Place the apples around the platter and garnish with pastries. Serve.

Sole Normandy

Baked Orange Roughy

4 servings

4	orange roughy filets
1½ cups	(*375 mL*) sliced mushrooms
½ cup	(*125 mL*) grated medium Cheddar cheese
	salt and pepper

Preheat oven to 450°F (*230°C*).

Place filets on individual pieces of heavy-duty foil.

Top with raw mushroom slices and cheese. Sprinkle with salt and pepper.

Wrap each filet tightly and place on a baking sheet.

Bake in oven 10 to 12 minutes.

Broiled Orange Roughy Parmesan

4 servings

4	orange roughy filets
¼ cup	(*60 mL*) melted butter
	salt and pepper
½ cup	(*125 mL*) grated Parmesan cheese

Place filets in a shallow baking pan, drizzle with half the melted butter, and season with salt and pepper.

Place under a heated broiler 3 to 4 minutes.

Turn filets over and drizzle with remaining butter.

Sprinkle with cheese and return to oven for 3-4 minutes or until cooked through and fish flakes with a fork.

Fennel Orange Roughy

4 servings

1 tbsp	(*15 mL*) crushed fennel seeds
½ cup	(*125 mL*) flour
¼ cup	(*60 mL*) light cream
3 tbsp	(*45 mL*) butter
4	orange roughy filets, 6 oz (*170 g*) each

Mix the fennel with the flour.

Dip the filets in the cream and dust with flour.

Heat the butter in a skillet.

Sauté the filets 2½ minutes each side.

Peppered Orange Roughy and Lime Butter

6 servings

6	orange roughy filets
2 tbsp	(*30 mL*) oil
2 tbsp	(*30 mL*) crushed dried green peppercorns
2 tbsp	(*30 mL*) cracked black peppercorns
2 tbsp	(*30 mL*) cracked white peppercorns
¼ cup	(*60 mL*) butter

Lime Butter

½ cup	(*125 mL*) softened butter
1 tbsp	(*15 mL*) grated lime rind
2 tbsp	(*30 mL*) lime juice
1	garlic clove, minced

Brush the fish with oil. Mix the peppercorns and coat each side of fish with pepper mixture.

Heat butter and gently sauté fish.

To prepare Lime Butter, combine butter with other ingredients.

Place on wax paper and roll. Refrigerate until firm.

Once fish is cooked, slice butter and place a slice on each filet.

1 Brush the fish filets with oil and coat each side with mixed peppercorns.

2 To make Lime Butter, combine butter with lime rind, lime juice and garlic.

3 Place on wax paper, roll and refrigerate until firm.

4 Once fish is cooked, slice butter and place a slice on each filet.

Dill Swordfish

6 servings

6	swordfish steaks
1 tbsp	(*15 mL*) oil
2 tbsp	(*30 mL*) dill weed
¼ cup	(*60 mL*) butter
1 tsp	(*5 mL*) lemon juice

Brush steaks with oil.

Broil the steaks 5 minutes each side, for each inch (*2,5 cm*) of thickness, (over coals is best).

Blend together the dill, butter and lemon juice.

Brush onto steaks as they grill and just before serving.

Grilled Swordfish with Walnut Sauce

Grilled Swordfish with Walnut Sauce

4 servings

4	swordfish steaks, 6 oz (*170 g*) each
1 tbsp	(*15 mL*) melted butter

Sauce

1 tsp	(*5 mL*) Dijon mustard
2 tsp	(*10 mL*) lemon juice
pinch	salt
¼ tsp	(*1 mL*) fresh cracked pepper
2 tbsp	(*30 mL*) walnut oil
¼ cup	(*60 mL*) olive oil

Brush fish with butter.

Grill in an oven broiler or over coals 4 minutes each side.

To prepare sauce, blend together the mustard, lemon juice, salt, pepper and oils thoroughly.

Brush fish with sauce and serve.

Whitefish Rolls

Whitefish Rolls

6 servings

3	slices bacon
1	carrot, finely diced
1	celery stalk, finely diced
1	small onion, finely diced
1 cup	(*250 mL*) grated Havarti cheese
6	whitefish filets
2 tbsp	(*30 mL*) butter
2 cups	(*500 mL*) Mornay Sauce

Preheat oven to 350°F (*180°C*).

Finely dice the bacon and sauté.

Add the vegetables and sauté until tender. Allow to cool.

Combine sautéed mixture with cheese.

Press cheese mixture onto each filet and roll.

Bake in a buttered pan for 15 to 20 minutes.

Remove from oven, place on plates and cover with heated Mornay Sauce.

Trout Jodee

2 servings

2	small trout
3 tbsp	(*45 mL*) butter
3 tbsp	(*45 mL*) oil
2	carrots, cut in julienne
1	zucchini, cut in julienne
2	celery stalks, cut in julienne
1 cup	(*250 mL*) commercial oyster sauce
½ lb	(*225 g*) oyster mushrooms
¼ cup	(*60 mL*) butter

Sauté the trout in the butter and oil, 4 to 5 minutes each side.

Remove from heat and keep hot.

Blanch the carrots, zucchini and celery for 5 minutes. Heat the sauce.

Sauté the vegetables and mushrooms in butter.

Place on a plate, top with trout and pour sauce over fish.

Bass Amandine

4 servings

¼ cup	(60 mL)	butter
4	bass filets, 6 oz (170 g) each	
¼ cup	(60 mL)	milk
¼ cup	(60 mL)	flour
⅓ cup	(80 mL)	slivered blanched almonds
1	lemon	

Heat the butter in a skillet.

Dip the bass in the milk then dust with flour.

Fry 2½ to 3 minutes each side. Remove fish to a heated platter.

Add almonds to butter and sauté until browned.

Squeeze the juice from the lemon into the butter. Swirl.

Pour over fish and serve.

Baked Red Snapper with Crab Stuffing

8 servings

¼ cup	(60 mL)	butter
1	small onion, minced	
½ tsp	(3 mL)	basil
1 tbsp	(15 mL)	chopped parsley
½ cup	(125 mL)	heavy cream
½ lb	(225 g)	crab meat
2 cups	(500 mL)	diced bread
3 tbsp	(45 mL)	lemon juice
5 lb	(2,2 kg)	red snapper

Preheat oven to 400°F (200°C).

In a saucepan, heat the butter.

Add the onion and sauté until tender.

In a mixing bowl, combine the remaining stuffing ingredients. Add to the butter and onion. Mix well.

Stuff into the fish. Tie together. Place in a baking pan.

Cover tail with tin foil so it won't burn.

Bake in oven 45 to 50 minutes.

Monkfish en Brochette

4 servings

1½ lbs	(675 g)	monkfish filets
3 tbsp	(45 mL)	oil
½ tsp	(3 mL)	basil
½ tsp	(3 mL)	thyme
½ tsp	(3 mL)	oregano
½ tsp	(3 mL)	salt
1 tbsp	(15 mL)	minced garlic
1 tsp	(5 mL)	parsley flakes
1½ tsp	(8 mL)	lemon juice
⅓ cup	(80 mL)	softened butter

Dice filets into 1-in. (2,5 cm) cubes.

Mix oil with basil, thyme, oregano and salt in a mixing bowl. Add fish.

Stir to cover fish with seasoned oil.

Blend the garlic, parsley and lemon juice into butter.

Skewer fish cubes with wooden (bamboo) skewers.

Broil in oven 5 minutes each side, brushing with butter.

Serve on rice.

Halibut with Rémoulade Sauce

Halibut with Rémoulade Sauce

4 servings

4	halibut steaks, 6 oz (170 g) each
1 tbsp	(15 mL) melted butter
3	egg yolks
¾ cup	(180 mL) oil
2 tbsp	(30 mL) fresh chopped parsley
1	garlic clove, minced
2	green onions, diced
1 tsp	(5 mL) paprika
3	drops Tabasco sauce

Heat the broiler (oven or gas).

Brush the halibut with butter.

Broil 4 minutes each side.

In a food processor with steel blades, blend the eggs. Slowly pour in the oil. Blend in the parsley, garlic, onions and seasonings; combine well.

Remove steaks and place on a platter.

Drop 1 tbsp (15 mL) of sauce in the center of each steak.

Serve with the remaining sauce.

Cod Soufflé

4 servings

1 tbsp	(15 mL) flour
¼ cup	(60 mL) heavy cream
1 tbsp	(15 mL) butter
1	egg
1	egg white
pinch	salt
⅛ tsp	(0,5 mL) cream of tartar
⅓ cup	(80 mL) cooked, flaked cod
½ cup	(125 mL) grated Parmesan cheese

Preheat oven to 350°F (180°C).

Blend the flour with a little of the cream into a paste.

Heat remaining cream and butter together until butter melts. Pour flour paste into cream. Stir until boiling. Remove from heat.

Whip the egg. Blend a little hot cream into the egg. Stir into sauce.

Beat the egg white with the salt and cream of tartar until stiff. Stir one quarter of the egg white into the sauce. Fold in the fish.

Add the remaining egg white in a folding motion. Try not to lose too much of the lightness of the egg white.

Fold into a greased casserole dish, which has been dusted with the grated cheese.

Bake in a water bath in oven for 35 minutes or until golden brown.

English-Style Fish

8 servings

1 cup	(250 mL) flour
½ tsp	(3 mL) baking powder
⅛ tsp	(0,5 mL) baking soda
¾ tsp	(4 mL) salt
pinch	white pepper
1 cup	(250 mL) beer
4 cups	(1 L) vegetable oil
1	egg white
2 lbs	(900 g) cod filet, cut into ¾-in. (2 cm) strips

In a mixing bowl, sift together all the dry ingredients.

Slowly add the beer. Whisk briskly. Let stand for 1½ hours.

Heat the oil to 375°F (190°C).

Whip the egg white. Fold into batter.

Dip fish into batter, allowing any excess batter to run off.

Using a slotted spoon, place fish in hot oil. Fry 2½ to 3 minutes or until golden brown.

Remove and keep hot on a paper towel-lined platter.

Pike Baked in Cream

4 servings

1 lb	(450 g) pike filets
3 tbsp	(45 mL) butter
1	small onion, diced
½	green pepper, diced
1	celery stalk, diced
½ cup	(125 mL) tomatoes, peeled, seeded and chopped
1½ cups	(375 mL) heavy cream
1 cup	(250 mL) grated Swiss cheese
½ cup	(125 mL) breadcrumbs
½ tsp	(3 mL) salt

Preheat oven to 350°F (180°C).

Wash and dry the fish. Place fish in a greased casserole dish.

Heat the butter in a saucepan.

Add the onion, pepper and celery; sauté until tender.

Add the tomatoes and simmer until liquid has evaporated. Spoon over fish.

Add the cream and sprinkle with cheese and breadcrumbs.

Bake in oven for 30 minutes.

Perch Filets with Shrimp Sauce

4 servings

1 lb	(450 g) perch filets
1 cup	(250 mL) flour
1	egg
½ cup	(125 mL) milk
1½ cups	(375 mL) fine breadcrumbs
3 tbsp	(45 mL) butter
3 tbsp	(45 mL) flour
1 cup	(250 mL) heavy cream
½ cup	(125 mL) fish stock (see *Soups*)
¼ cup	(60 mL) sherry
½ tsp	(3 mL) salt
½ lb	(225 g) baby shrimp
1 cup	(250 mL) oil

Wash and dry the filets. Dust with flour.

Mix the egg with the milk. Dip filets in egg mixture. Dredge with breadcrumbs. Reserve.

Heat the butter in a saucepan. Add 3 tbsp (45 mL) flour and stir into a paste (roux). Cook for 2 minutes.

Add the cream, stock and sherry. Simmer until thick.

Add the salt and shrimp. Simmer for 5 minutes.

Heat oil in a large skillet.

Fry the fish in the oil 1½ to 2 minutes each side.

Place on a platter. Pour half the sauce over the fish. Serve the remainder separately.

Perch Filets with Eggs and Brown Butter

Perch Filets with Eggs and Brown Butter

3 servings

4 cups	(1 L) court bouillon (see *Soups*)
1 lb	(450 g) perch filets
⅓ cup	(80 mL) butter
1 tsp	(5 mL) parsley flakes
1½ tsp	(8 mL) lemon juice
2	hard-boiled eggs, chopped

Heat court bouillon. Gently simmer the fish in the court bouillon for 6 minutes.

In a saucepan, heat the butter until it turns hazelnut-brown in color.

Add the parsley and lemon juice.

Place fish on a serving platter. Pour butter over fish.

Sprinkle with chopped eggs.

Three-Pepper Prawns

8 servings

2 tbsp	*(30 mL)* oil
¼ cup	*(60 mL)* butter
2	garlic cloves, crushed
2 tbsp	*(30 mL)* green peppercorns
2 tbsp	*(30 mL)* cracked black pepper
1 tsp	*(5 mL)* cayenne pepper
3 lbs	*(1,3 kg)* prawns, shelled and deveined
½ cup	*(125 mL)* red pimiento
1 tsp	*(5 mL)* sugar
2 tbsp	*(30 mL)* brandy

Heat the oil and butter in a large frying pan.

Add the garlic and peppers and sauté 2 minutes.

Add the prawns and sauté until tender. Stir in pimiento.

Sprinkle with sugar and flame with brandy. Serve at once.

Three-Pepper Prawns

Shrimp Aïoli

4 servings

4 cups	*(1 L)* court bouillon, (see *Soups*)
1 lb	*(450 g)* prawns, peeled and deveined
4	garlic cloves, pressed
1½ tsp	*(8 mL)* vinegar
2 tbsp	*(30 mL)* breadcrumbs
pinch	salt
1	egg yolk
¾ cup	*(180 mL)* olive oil

Bring court bouillon to a boil. Cook the shrimp in the court bouillon for 3 to 4 minutes. Remove and chill.

Place garlic in blender. Add vinegar and breadcrumbs. Blend for 30 seconds.

Add the salt and egg yolk and blend until smooth. With blender running, slowly pour in the oil. Blend into a thick sauce.

Place shrimp on a platter. Serve with sauce in the center.

Shrimp à l'Étouffée

Shrimp à l'Étouffée

6 servings

½ cup	(*125 mL*) butter
1	onion, diced
1	green pepper, diced
2¼ lbs	(*1 kg*) shrimp, peeled and deveined
2 cups	(*500 mL*) tomato sauce
1 tsp	(*5 mL*) salt
1 tsp	(*5 mL*) pepper
1 tsp	(*5 mL*) paprika
½ tsp	(*3 mL*) oregano
½ tsp	(*3 mL*) thyme
½ tsp	(*3 mL*) cayenne pepper
½ tsp	(*3 mL*) garlic powder
½ tsp	(*3 mL*) white pepper
3 tbsp	(*45 mL*) diced green onions
1 tbsp	(*15 mL*) parsley flakes

Melt the butter and sauté the onion and green pepper.

Add the shrimp and cook gently.

Add the tomato sauce and seasonings. Simmer, half-covered, for 20 minutes.

Stir in the green onions and parsley flakes.

Serve over noodles or rice.

Tempura Shrimp

6 servings

½ cup	(125 mL)	milk
2¾ cups	(680 mL)	flour
2 tbsp	(30 mL)	cornstarch
1 tsp	(5 mL)	baking powder
1 tsp	(5 mL)	salt
2		eggs, beaten
4 cups	(1 L)	oil
2¼ lbs	(1 kg)	prawns, peeled and deveined

Blend the milk, ¾ cup (180 mL) flour, cornstarch, baking powder, salt, eggs and 2 tbsp (30 mL) oil into a smooth batter.

Heat the remaining oil to 375°F (190°C).

Dip the shrimp into the remaining flour, then into the batter.

Cook in the oil 2½ to 3 minutes. Serve hot.

Jumbo Fantail Shrimp

8 servings

2¼ lbs	(1 kg)	large shrimp, peeled and deveined
2 cups	(500 mL)	flour
½ cup	(125 mL)	cornmeal
1 tsp	(5 mL)	baking powder
1 tsp	(5 mL)	salt
½ tsp	(3 mL)	oregano
½ tsp	(3 mL)	thyme
½ tsp	(3 mL)	basil
1 tsp	(5 mL)	paprika
½ tsp	(3 mL)	pepper
2		eggs
1 cup	(250 mL)	heavy cream
4 cups	(1 L)	oil

Butterfly the shrimp.

Sift 1 cup (250 mL) of flour into cornmeal.

Add the baking powder and seasonings.

Beat the eggs into the cream. Stir into the seasoned flour.

Dust the shrimp with the remaining flour. Dip into batter.

Fry in the oil, which has been heated to 375°F (190°C). Serve at once.

B.B.Q. Shrimp

8 servings

3 lbs	(1,4 kg)	large shrimp
¼ cup	(60 mL)	butter
½ cup	(125 mL)	olive oil
1 tbsp	(15 mL)	Worcestershire sauce
4		garlic cloves, minced
4 tsp	(20 mL)	lemon juice
2 tsp	(10 mL)	chopped parsley
½ tsp	(3 mL)	paprika
½ tsp	(3 mL)	basil
½ tsp	(3 mL)	thyme
½ tsp	(3 mL)	oregano
½ tsp	(3 mL)	cayenne pepper
½ tsp	(3 mL)	hot pepper sauce
½ tsp	(3 mL)	salt

Place the shrimp in a large mixing bowl.

Add the remaining ingredients to a saucepan.

Combine well and heat without boiling, then chill. Pour over shrimp.

Marinate 30 minutes, stirring from time to time.

Preheat oven to 325°F (160°C).

Pour shrimp and sauce on a baking sheet; bake 8 to 10 minutes in oven.

Serve at once.

Jumbo Stuffed Shrimp

4 servings

2 tbsp	(*30 mL*) butter
1 tbsp	(*15 mL*) minced green onion
1 tbsp	(*15 mL*) Dijon mustard
1 tsp	(*5 mL*) chopped sage
1 cup	(*250 mL*) breadcrumbs
1 cup	(*250 mL*) crab meat
1	egg
¼ cup	(*60 mL*) heavy cream
24	large prawns, butterflied

Preheat oven to 425°F (*220°C*).

In 2 tsp (*10 mL*) butter, sauté the onion. Blend in the mustard and sage. Remove from heat.

In a mixing bowl, blend together the breadcrumbs, crab meat, egg, cream, sage mixture and remaining butter.

Place 2 tbsp (*30 mL*) of mixture on each butterflied shrimp. Place on a lightly greased baking sheet.

Bake in oven 8 to 10 minutes, or until golden brown. Serve hot.

1

Sauté the green onion in 2 tsp (*10 mL*) butter; blend in the mustard and sage and remove from heat.

2

Blend together the breadcrumbs, crab meat, egg, cream, sage mixture and remaining butter.

3

Place 2 tbsp (*30 mL*) of mixture on each butterflied shrimp.

4

Bake in oven 8 to 10 minutes, or until golden brown.

Shrimp Creole au Gratin

4-6 servings

3 cups	(*750 mL*) court bouillon (see *Soups*)
1½ lbs	(*675 g*) large fresh shrimp
2 cups	(*500 mL*) cooked and drained fettuccine noodles
1½ cups	(*375 mL*) Creole Sauce
½ cup	(*125 mL*) coarsely grated medium Cheddar cheese
½ cup	(*125 mL*) coarsely grated old Cheddar cheese
½ cup	(*125 mL*) coarsely grated Swiss or Havarti cheese

Preheat oven to 400°F (*200°C*).

Bring court bouillon to a boil. Add shrimp and simmer just until cooked through, about 3 to 5 minutes.

Cool, peel, and devein shrimp.

Place noodles in a greased shallow baking dish. Spread shrimp over noodles; pour sauce evenly over shrimp.

Combine cheeses and sprinkle over sauce.

Bake in oven 25 to 30 minutes or until the cheese is melted and golden.

Coquilles St. Jacques à l'Indienne

4 servings

1 cup	(*250 mL*) white wine
1 lb	(*450 g*) scallops
¼ cup	(*60 mL*) butter
1	small onion, diced
1	green pepper, diced
1	celery stalk, diced
3 tbsp	(*45 mL*) flour
1 cup	(*250 mL*) heavy cream
⅓ cup	(*80 mL*) sherry
½ tsp	(*3 mL*) salt
2 tsp	(*10 mL*) curry powder
1 cup	(*250 mL*) tomatoes, peeled, seeded and chopped

Heat the wine. Add the scallops and cook for 6 minutes. Set aside.

In a saucepan, heat the butter. Sauté the vegetables until tender.

Add the flour and stir. Cook for 2 minutes.

Add the cream, sherry and seasonings. Simmer until thickened.

Add the tomatoes and scallops. Simmer for 5 minutes.

Coquilles St. Jacques Florentine

2 servings

10 oz	(*284 g*) spinach
1 tbsp	(*15 mL*) butter
1 cup	(*250 mL*) white wine
½ lb	(*225 g*) scallops
1 cup	(*250 mL*) Mornay Sauce (see *Sauces*)
¼ cup	(*60 mL*) grated Parmesan cheese

Preheat oven to 450°F (*230°C*).

Clean and stem the spinach. Cook in boiling, salted water for 5 minutes. Drain. Cool.

Coarsely chop the spinach.

Heat butter in a skillet. Add spinach and sauté 3 minutes.

Place spinach in a greased casserole dish.

Heat wine. Add scallops and cook for 6 minutes. Remove and place on spinach.

Cover with Mornay Sauce. Sprinkle with Parmesan.

Place in oven 3 to 5 minutes or until golden brown.

Coquilles St. Jacques à l'Indienne and Coquilles St. Jacques Florentine

Paprika Scallops

4 servings

3 tbsp	*(45 mL)* butter
1 lb	*(450 g)* scallops
3 tbsp	*(45 mL)* flour
1 cup	*(250 mL)* heavy cream
¼ cup	*(60 mL)* sherry
1 tbsp	*(15 mL)* Hungarian paprika
3	green onions, minced

Heat the butter in a large skillet. Add the scallops and sauté for 5 minutes.

Sprinkle in the flour. Cook 2 minutes. Add the cream, sherry and paprika.

Reduce heat and simmer 8 to 10 minutes or until thickened.

Sprinkle with green onions. Serve over rice or fettuccine.

Coquilles St. Jacques Meunière

8 servings

2 lbs	*(900 g)* scallops
1 tsp	*(5 mL)* salt
½ tsp	*(3 mL)* pepper
½ tsp	*(3 mL)* paprika
2 cups	*(500 mL)* flour
1½ cups	*(375 mL)* milk
4 cups	*(1 L)* oil
½ cup	*(125 mL)* butter
1 tbsp	*(15 mL)* parsley
2 tsp	*(10 mL)* lemon juice

Paprika Scallops

Wash and dry the scallops. Mix the seasonings into the flour.

Heat oil to 375°F *(190°C)*. Dip scallops in milk, then into seasoned flour.

Fry in the oil to golden brown. Place in a serving dish.

Slowly cook the butter until it turns to a hazelnut-brown color.

Sprinkle with parsley and lemon juice. Pour over scallops and serve.

Scallops au Gratin

Meanwhile, sauté mushrooms in butter over high heat.

Stir mushrooms and shrimp into Mornay Sauce.

Place scallops in 4 individual shells or baking dishes.

Spoon sauce mixture over and sprinkle with grated cheeses.

Place under heated broiler until cheese melts.

Kentucky Scallops

8 servings

2 lbs	(900 g)	scallops
½ tsp	(3 mL)	oregano
½ tsp	(3 mL)	thyme
½ tsp	(3 mL)	basil
½ tsp	(3 mL)	garlic powder
½ tsp	(3 mL)	onion powder
½ tsp	(3 mL)	paprika
½ tsp	(3 mL)	pepper
1 tsp	(5 mL)	salt
2 cups	(500 mL)	flour
4 cups	(1 L)	oil
1½ cups	(375 mL)	milk

Wash the scallops, then dry them. Blend all the seasonings into the flour.

Heat the oil to 375°F (190°C).

Dip scallops in milk then into the seasoned flour.

Deep fry in the oil 2 to 3 minutes or until golden brown.

Scallops au Gratin

4 servings

1 lb	(450 g)	scallops
		court bouillon (see *Soups*) or salted water
1½ cups	(375 mL)	sliced mushrooms
2 tbsp	(30 mL)	butter
½ cup	(125 mL)	cooked baby shrimp
2 cups	(500 mL)	Mornay Sauce
½ cup	(125 mL)	grated mild Cheddar cheese
½ cup	(125 mL)	grated mozzarella cheese
¾ cup	(180 mL)	grated Parmesan cheese

Place scallops in a medium saucepan and cover with court bouillon or water.

Bring to a simmer and cook 3 to 5 minutes or until scallops are cooked through; drain.

Sylvia's Jumbo Crab Claws

8 servings

2 tbsp	*(30 mL)*	butter
2¼ cups	*(560 mL)*	flour
1 cup	*(250 mL)*	milk
4 cups	*(1 L)*	crab meat, cooked
½ tsp	*(3 mL)*	thyme
½ tsp	*(3 mL)*	basil
½ tsp	*(3 mL)*	oregano
½ tsp	*(3 mL)*	pepper
1 tsp	*(5 mL)*	paprika
1 tsp	*(5 mL)*	salt
2		eggs
1 cup	*(250 mL)*	milk
3 cups	*(750 mL)*	fine breadcrumbs
4 cups	*(1 L)*	oil

Heat the butter in a saucepan. Add ¼ cup *(60 mL)* of flour and stir. Cook two minutes.

Add 1 cup *(250 mL)* milk and cook very slowly over low heat until very thick. Cool.

Add the crab meat and blend.

Shape into 8 crab claws. Place on a wax paper-lined pastry sheet.

Chill in refrigerator for 2 hours.

Blend the seasonings with the remaining flour. Beat the eggs and add the milk. Dust crab claws with seasoned flour and dip into eggs. Dredge with breadcrumbs.

Heat oil to 375°F *(180°C)*. Fry one or two claws at a time until golden brown.

Serve at once.

1

Add crab meat to thickened, cooled milk.

2

Shape into 8 crab claws.

3

Dust claws with seasoned flour, dip into eggs and dredge with breadcrumbs.

4

Fry one or two claws at a time in heated oil until golden brown.

Crab Louis

Add cream and simmer, stirring, until thickened. Stir in crab meat and season to taste.

Spoon hot mixture into a greased shallow baking dish. Sprinkle with almonds and cheese. Bake in oven just until cheese is golden.

Crab Louis

4 servings

1 lb	(*450 g*) crab meat
2	heads butter lettuce
3	tomatoes, sliced
4	hard-boiled eggs, quartered
16	green olives

Sauce

¾ cup	(*180 mL*) chili sauce
½ cup	(*125 mL*) mayonnaise
1 tsp	(*5 mL*) minced onion
½ tsp	(*3 mL*) sugar
¼ tsp	(*1 mL*) Worcestershire sauce
¼ tsp	(*1 mL*) salt
pinch	pepper

Check crab meat and remove any cartilage. On four plates, arrange the lettuce leaves. Place 4 oz (*115 g*) of crab meat in the center of lettuce. Place 4 slices of tomato and egg around the crab meat. Pour over 2 tbsp (*30 mL*) of sauce. Garnish with the olives. Serve remaining sauce separately.

Sauce : Blend together all the ingredients thoroughly. Chill 30 minutes before serving.

Baked Crab au Gratin

6-8 servings

1	medium onion, chopped
1	green pepper, chopped
1	red pepper, chopped
8	large mushrooms, sliced
2	large tomatoes, peeled, seeded and diced
¼ cup	(*60 mL*) butter
¼ cup	(*60 mL*) all-purpose flour
1¼ cups	(*310 mL*) heavy cream
2¼ lbs	(*1 kg*) cooked crab meat
	salt and pepper
¼ cup	(*60 mL*) sliced almonds
2 cups	(*500 mL*) grated medium Cheddar cheese

Preheat oven to 450°F (*230°C*).

Sauté the vegetables in butter until tender. Sprinkle with flour; stir until well blended.

Lobster Mornay

4 servings

4	live lobsters, about 1½ lbs (675 g) each
	court bouillon (see *Soups*)
3 tbsp	(45 mL) finely chopped onion
3 tbsp	(45 mL) finely chopped celery
3 tbsp	(45 mL) finely chopped carrot
8	large mushrooms, sliced
2 tbsp	(30 mL) butter
1 cup	(250 mL) cooked diced chicken
1¾ cups	(430 mL) Mornay Sauce (see *Sauces*)
1 cup	(250 mL) grated Swiss cheese

Holding lobsters by the back, plunge them, head first, into a large pot of boiling court bouillon.

Simmer 12 to 15 minutes, or until lobsters rise to the surface. Drain.

Sauté the vegetables in butter. Stir in the chicken and hot Mornay Sauce. Simmer over low heat until mixture is thickened.

Slice lobsters in half horizontally, crack claws, and remove all lobster meat and tamale or coral roe.

Discard the claws. Slice lobster meat and stir into the Mornay mixture with tamale or roe; spoon mixture into the half shells and tail.

Sprinkle with cheese and place under heated broiler until golden.

Lobster Thermidor

6 servings

3	lobsters, 1½ lbs (675 g) each
¼ cup	(60 mL) butter
2 tbsp	(30 mL) oil
3	shallots, chopped
¼ cup	(60 mL) white wine
¼ cup	(60 mL) sherry
2 cups	(500 mL) Mornay Sauce (see *Sauces*)
1 tbsp	(15 mL) parsley
1 tsp	(5 mL) dry mustard
1 tbsp	(15 mL) heavy cream
½ cup	(125 mL) grated Parmesan cheese

Preheat oven to 400°F (200°C).

Split the lobsters in half. Remove and crack the claws.

Melt 2 tbsp (30 mL) butter and drizzle over the lobster.

Pour oil on large pastry sheet. Place lobster and claws on pastry sheet. Place in oven for 10 minutes.

While lobster is cooking, heat remaining butter in a saucepan.

Add shallots and simmer until tender. Add wine and sherry and reduce to ¼ cup (60 mL).

Add the Mornay Sauce, parsley and dry mustard. Cook 3 minutes on high heat, stirring constantly with a whisk.

Remove lobster from oven. Take meat out of shells. Reserve shells.

Dice the meat and place in a mixing bowl. Add ⅔ of the sauce. Combine. Spoon a little of the sauce into the shells. Fill shells with lobster mixture.

Pour remaining sauce and cream over mixture. Sprinkle with cheese.

Return to oven and brown. Serve.

Lobster Medallions in Pernod Cream

6 servings

6	lobster tails
1	small onion, minced
1	garlic clove, minced
1 tbsp	(15 mL) butter
2 cups	(500 mL) crushed tomatoes
1 tsp	(5 mL) fennel seeds
¼ cup	(60 mL) Pernod
½ cup	(125 mL) heavy cream

Cut the lobster tails into medallions.

Sauté the onion and garlic in the butter until tender.

Add the tomatoes, fennel seeds and Pernod; simmer for 12 minutes.

Add the cream and lobster and simmer 10 more minutes. Serve at once.

Lobster Henri Duvernois

Lobster Henri Duvernois

6 servings

2¼ lbs	(1 kg)	lobster meat
¼ cup	(60 mL)	butter
½ cup	(125 mL)	leeks, julienned
⅔ cup	(160 mL)	sherry
2 tbsp	(30 mL)	brandy
2 cups	(500 mL)	heavy cream
4 cups	(1 L)	cooked rice, hot

Sauté the lobster meat in the butter. Add the leeks and cook until tender.

Add the sherry and brandy and simmer for 5 minutes.

Remove lobster and keep hot.

Add cream and reduce to half the volume.

Place lobster over rice, pour sauce over the lobster and serve.

Pamela's Seafood Sloppy Joes

6 servings

¼ cup	(60 mL) oil
2	garlic cloves, minced
1	small onion, finely diced
1	green pepper, finely diced
4 oz	(115 g) mushrooms, sliced
2	celery stalks, minced
1 lb	(450 g) small shrimp, peeled and deveined
2 cups	(500 mL) tomato purée
¼ tsp	(1 mL) oregano
¼ tsp	(1 mL) thyme leaves
¼ tsp	(1 mL) basil
¼ tsp	(1 mL) chili powder
¼ tsp	(1 mL) paprika
¼ tsp	(1 mL) pepper
1 tsp	(5 mL) salt
1 lb	(450 g) crab meat, cooked
1	french loaf, cut into 6 thick slices
2 cups	(500 mL) grated Cheddar cheese

Heat the oil in a large skillet. Add the garlic, onion, pepper, mushrooms and celery; sauté until tender.

Add the shrimp; cook until pink. Add the tomato purée and seasonings; stir. Cook for 10 minutes over low heat.

Add the crab meat and simmer for 5 more minutes.

Hollow the sliced bread to form a cavity. Place bread under oven broiler and toast.

Remove and fill the bread cavity with seafood mixture.

Sprinkle with cheese and return under the broiler for 1 minute or until browned.

Seafood Crêpes Mornay

8 servings

Crêpes

3	eggs
¼ tsp	(1 mL) salt
1 cup	(250 mL) milk
¾ cup	(180 mL) flour
3 tbsp	(45 mL) butter

Filling

¼ cup	(60 mL) butter
1 cup	(250 mL) tiny scallops
1 cup	(250 mL) baby shrimp
1 cup	(250 mL) crab meat, cooked
2 cups	(500 mL) Mornay Sauce (see *Sauces*)
2 cups	(500 mL) grated Cheddar cheese

Crêpes : Whip the eggs until very light. Add the salt and milk. Fold in the flour a little at a time.

Lightly grease a heated skillet with a little butter. Pour in enough batter to cover the bottom of the pan.

Rotate the pan to spread the batter into a thin layer.

Grill the crêpe until browned. Turn over, grill 30 seconds and remove to a plate.

Filling : Preheat oven to 350°F (180°C).

Heat the butter in a saucepan. Add the scallops and sauté.

Add the shrimp and crab meat. Simmer for 3 minutes.

Stir in the sauce. Simmer for 5 minutes.

Spoon 3 tbsp (45 mL) of seafood mixture onto each crêpe. Roll crêpes.

Place crêpes in a greased casserole dish. Sprinkle with cheese.

Bake in oven for 15 minutes.

Seafood Crêpes Mornay

Lobster Crab Casserole

4 servings

1 cup	(*250 mL*) crab meat, cooked
1 cup	(*250 mL*) lobster meat, cooked
1/2 cup	(*125 mL*) finely diced celery
1	green pepper, finely diced
1	onion, finely diced
3/4 cup	(*180 mL*) mayonnaise
1/2 tsp	(*3 mL*) salt
1/4 tsp	(*1 mL*) pepper
1/2 tsp	(*3 mL*) paprika
1 tsp	(*5 mL*) Worcestershire sauce
1/2 cup	(*125 mL*) breadcrumbs
1/2 cup	(*125 mL*) grated Cheddar cheese

Preheat oven to 350°F (*180°C*).

Combine the seafood with the vegetables. Stir in the mayonnaise and seasonings.

Scrape mixture into a greased casserole.

Sprinkle with breadcrumbs and cheese. Bake in oven for 30 minutes.

Escargots à la Bourguignonne

8 servings

48	snails, canned
3 cups	(*750 mL*) court bouillon (see *Soups*)
1 3/4 cups	(*430 mL*) softened butter
3	garlic cloves, crushed
1 cup	(*250 mL*) chopped fresh parsley
2 tsp	(*10 mL*) black pepper
1 tbsp	(*15 mL*) brandy
48	snail shells

Preheat oven to 400°F (*200°C*).

Gently simmer the snails in the court bouillon for 30 minutes.

While snails are cooking, blend the butter, garlic, parsley, pepper and brandy together.

Drain the snails and stuff into shells. Fill each shell with butter mixture.

Bake in oven for 5 minutes. Serve with garlic bread.

John Hoyle's Fresh Oysters

3-6 servings

36	fresh New Orleans oysters
2	green onions, minced
1/3 cup	(*80 mL*) red wine vinegar
1 tsp	(*5 mL*) lemon juice
3	lemons, quartered

Scrub and shuck the oysters. Detach the bivalve from the shell. Leave in the larger shell. Discard the top shell.

Blend the green onions, vinegar and lemon juice together.

Place oysters on a serving platter. Spoon 1/2 tsp (*3 mL*) of sauce on each oyster.

Serve with lemons.

Oysters Bienville

Oysters Bienville

4 servings

2 tbsp	(30 mL) butter
3 oz	(90 g) mushrooms, sliced
3	green onions, diced
2 tbsp	(30 mL) flour
2/3 cup	(160 mL) fish stock (see *Soups*)
1/3 cup	(80 mL) sherry
1/2 tsp	(3 mL) salt
pinch	cayenne pepper
1	egg yolk
24	oysters on the half shell
1/2 cup	(125 mL) fine breadcrumbs
2 tbsp	(30 mL) grated Parmesan cheese

Preheat oven to 400°F (200°C).

In a saucepan, heat the butter. Sauté the mushrooms and green onions.

Add the flour, stir and cook 2 minutes. Add the fish stock, sherry and seasonings. Simmer for 5 minutes.

Whip the egg yolk. Stir into sauce. Cook for 5 minutes over low heat.

Place oysters on a baking sheet. Bake in oven 5 minutes.

Remove from oven and top with sauce. Sprinkle with breadcrumbs and cheese.

Return to oven and bake until golden brown. Serve at once.

Pasta

There's much more to pasta than spaghetti with tomato sauce. In fact, pasta has been around a lot longer than the tomato, which Europeans only discovered during one of their 16th century forays to South America. Legend has it that Marco Polo brought pasta back from the Orient, but chances are, it was around even before that.

You'll find a wide choice of pasta recipes in this chapter, but few of them involve tomatoes. Pasta seems to pair up wonderfully with almost everything — meat, seafood, vegetables, any number of cheeses.

Once you get used to preparing different types of pasta dishes, you'll find that you will be able to improvise with ingredients you have on hand and create new recipes of your very own.

You might even want to try making your own pasta. A basic recipe for pasta dough is included. Once you master it, you can vary it by adding fresh herbs, spinach or tomato purée to make colored pastas.

Once you have rolled out your homemade pasta dough, you can cut it to the desired shape. It's easy to make your own lasagne or fettucine noodles and you can even make your own ravioli.

But you can also buy many good brands of commercially-made pasta in wonderful and exotic shapes, with names to match. Don't be afraid to experiment.

Fettuccine Primavera

Fettuccine Primavera

8 servings

¼ lb	(115 g) broccoli florets
¼ lb	(115 g) cauliflower florets
¼ cup	(60 mL) butter
1	small onion, finely diced
1	small carrot, finely diced
3 oz	(90 g) mushrooms, sliced
¼ cup	(60 mL) flour
3 cups	(750 mL) light cream
2 tbsp	(30 mL) pimiento, finely diced
½ cup	(125 mL) grated Parmesan cheese
1 tsp	(5 mL) cracked black pepper
1 lb	(450 g) fettuccine

Blanch the broccoli and cauliflower in boiling water. Drain and set aside.

Heat the butter in a saucepan; sauté the onion, carrot and mushrooms until tender.

Add the flour and stir. Cook for 2 minutes. Add the cream, broccoli and cauliflower.

Reduce to a simmer. Simmer 15 minutes.

Add the pimiento, Parmesan and pepper.

Cook the noodles al dente in a pot of boiling, salted water. Drain.

Place noodles in a large serving bowl. Pour sauce over and serve.

Basic Pasta Dough

8 servings

4 cups	(1 L)	flour
½ tsp	(3 mL)	salt
4		eggs
⅓ cup	(80 mL)	cold water

Sift the flour and salt together. Place in a mixing bowl. Mix on slow speed.

Add one egg at a time. Blend slightly after each addition.

Slowly add the water until a stiff dough is formed. Knead the dough for 10 minutes. Divide into 3 parts.

Wrap the dough in a damp cloth and allow it to rest for at least 30 minutes.*

To roll, use a lightly flour-dusted surface and rolling pin.

Roll the ball away from you, turning it one quarter of the way at a time and repeat rolling.

Roll out the dough to ⅛-in. (0,3 cm) thickness.

The dough is now ready for cutting or stuffing according to the recipe you are following.

The dough can be frozen at this point. Defrost dough in refrigerator overnight, then remove it to room temperature for 1 hour before using.

Pasta Topped with Cheese-Stuffed Tomatoes

6 servings

½ lb	(225 g)	penne noodles
6		tomatoes
1 tsp	(5 mL)	basil
½ tsp	(3 mL)	chervil
½ tsp	(3 mL)	oregano
¼ tsp	(1 mL)	pepper
½ tsp	(3 mL)	salt
¼ lb	(115 g)	grated mozzarella cheese
¼ lb	(115 g)	grated Cheddar cheese
½ cup	(125 mL)	grated Parmesan cheese
3 oz	(90 g)	butter

Preheat oven to 350°F (180°C).

Cook the noodles al dente in a large pot of boiling, salted water. Drain.

Plunge the tomatoes in boiling water for 1 minute. Remove and skin the tomatoes. Cut the tops from the tomatoes.

Carefully scoop out the centers and discard. Sprinkle centers with seasonings and pack with mozzarella and Cheddar.

Bake in oven until tomatoes are soft and cheese melts.

Place noodles on a large greased platter.

Top with the tomatoes. Sprinkle with Parmesan and dot with butter.

Return to oven for 5 minutes. Serve.

Pasta Ragu

8 cups (2 L)

½ lb	(225 g)	ground beef
½ lb	(225 g)	ground veal
¼ lb	(115 g)	ground bacon
1		onion, minced
1		carrot, minced
4 oz	(115 g)	mushrooms, sliced
1		garlic clove, minced
1		bouquet garni
1 tsp	(5 mL)	salt
4 cups	(1 L)	tomato purée
1½ cups	(375 mL)	water

Brown the beef, veal and bacon together.

Add the vegetables and sauté until tender.

Add the garlic, bouquet garni, salt, tomato purée and water.

Reduce heat to low and simmer for 2 hours, skimming off any fat that rises to the top.

Serve over your choice of cooked pasta.

Pasta Topped with Cheese-Stuffed Tomatoes

Fettuccine My Way

8 servings

1 lb	(*450 g*) fettuccine
1 lb	(*450 g*) large shrimp, sliced in halves
2	small onions, diced
½ cup	(*125 mL*) sliced mushrooms
1	green pepper, diced
¼ cup	(*60 mL*) olive oil
¼ cup	(*60 mL*) chopped, seeded tomatoes
2 tbsp	(*30 mL*) sliced black olives
1 cup	(*250 mL*) heavy cream
½ cup	(*125 mL*) grated Parmesan cheese
2 tsp	(*10 mL*) black pepper

In a large pot, cook the fettuccine in salted, boiling water until al dente.

Sauté the shrimp, onions, mushrooms and green pepper in the oil until tender. Add the tomatoes and olives and toss to heat.

Stir in the cream, cheese and pepper. Simmer until thick.

Toss the noodles with the sauce and serve at once.

Fettuccine Niagara

Fettuccine Niagara

8 servings

1 lb	(*450 g*) fettuccine
3 tbsp	(*45 mL*) butter
1 cup	(*250 mL*) diced apples
3 tbsp	(*45 mL*) flour
2 cups	(*500 mL*) heavy cream
¼ cup	(*60 mL*) white wine (very sweet)
1 cup	(*250 mL*) baby shrimp
1 cup	(*250 mL*) diced peaches or apricots

In a large pot, cook the fettuccine in boiling, salted water until al dente.

In a saucepan, heat the butter. Sauté the apples until tender.

Add the flour and stir into a paste (roux). Add the cream and wine. Simmer for 5 minutes. Add the shrimp and peaches.

Pour sauce over pasta. Serve at once.

Fettuccine with Scallops and Sherry

8 servings

1 lb	(*450 g*) fettuccine
1 lb	(*450 g*) baby scallops
1	onion, minced
1 cup	(*250 mL*) sliced mushrooms
½ cup	(*125 mL*) butter
2 cups	(*500 mL*) Béchamel Sauce (see *Sauces*)
½ cup	(*125 mL*) sherry
1	egg yolk, beaten
½ cup	(*125 mL*) fresh chopped parsley

Cook fettuccine al dente in a large pot of boiling, salted water.

Sauté the scallops, onion and mushrooms in the butter.

Add the Béchamel and sherry. Whisk in the egg yolk and simmer for 5 minutes.

Place noodles on plates and top with sauce. Garnish with parsley.

Fettuccine with Scallops and Sherry

Fettuccine with Smoked Chicken

8 servings

1	small onion, minced
½ lb	(*225 g*) boneless smoked chicken, diced
3 tbsp	(*45 mL*) olive oil
1½ cups	(*375 mL*) tomatoes, seeded and puréed
8 oz	(*250 g*) mascarpone (cream cheese)
pinch	sweet basil
1 lb	(*450 g*) cooked fettuccine noodles

Sauté the onion and chicken in the oil, add tomatoes and simmer until most of moisture has evaporated.

Sprinkle in mascarpone and basil.

Pour sauce over noodles and serve.

Cannelloni

8 servings

½	recipe basic pasta dough
¾ cup	(*180 mL*) grated Parmesan cheese
1 cup	(*250 mL*) ricotta cheese
½ cup	(*125 mL*) grated mozzarella cheese
½ cup	(*125 mL*) grated white Cheddar
8 oz	(*225 g*) butter
1 tbsp	(*15 mL*) chopped parsley
1 tsp	(*5 mL*) basil
1 tsp	(*5 mL*) thyme
1 tsp	(*5 mL*) oregano
1 tsp	(*5 mL*) salt
2	eggs
½ cup	(*125 mL*) breadcrumbs
⅓ cup	(*80 mL*) flour
2 cups	(*500 mL*) heavy cream
2 cups	(*500 mL*) chicken stock (see *Soups*)

Preheat oven to 350°F (*180°C*).

Roll out dough as instructed in basic pasta dough recipe. Cut into 4 x 6-in. (*10 x 15 cm*) rectangles.

Cook in boiling water for 1 minute. Remove and place on a cloth.

Blend together the cheeses, half the butter, seasonings, eggs and breadcrumbs thoroughly.

Place the filling evenly over pasta sheets. Roll and seal ends and bottom edge.

Place in a large greased casserole dish.

Melt the remaining butter in a saucepan. Stir in the flour and blend. Cook 2 minutes. Do not brown.

Add the cream and stock. Simmer until sauce thickens.

Pour sauce over pasta and bake for 30 minutes or until browned.

Fusilli with Cheese and Tomatoes

8 servings

¼ cup	(*60 mL*) olive oil
¾ lb	(*340 g*) tomatoes, seeded and chopped
2 tsp	(*10 mL*) oregano
1 tsp	(*5 mL*) chervil
1 tsp	(*5 mL*) thyme
1 tsp	(*5 mL*) salt
¼ tsp	(*1 mL*) pepper
1 lb	(*450 g*) fusilli
¼ cup	(*60 mL*) grated Romano cheese
½ lb	(*225 g*) grated mozzarella cheese

Heat the oil, add the tomatoes and cook, mashing into a purée with the seasonings.

Cook the noodles al dente in a pot of boiling, salted water. Drain.

Blend the hot noodles into the hot sauce. Stir in the cheeses and serve.

Gnocchi

6 servings

3	medium potatoes, mashed
1 cup	(*250 mL*) flour
1	egg
1 tsp	(*5 mL*) salt
¼ tsp	(*1 mL*) pepper

Place the hot mashed potatoes in a mixing bowl. Blend in the flour a little at a time.

Add the egg, salt and pepper. Beat until smooth.

Knead into a smooth, soft ball.

If dough is sticky, a little more flour can be added. Roll out the dough into long oblong shapes. Cut into ¾-in. (*2 cm*) pieces. With a floured fork, press each piece firmly.

Cook immediately or freeze, if desired.

To cook, boil water and a little salt. Drop gnocchi in a few at a time.

Cook five minutes, remove and serve with sauce of your choice such as Alfredo, Mornay, tomato or Bolognese.

Fusilli, Prosciutto and Mustard Sauce

Fusilli, Prosciutto and Mustard Sauce

8 servings

1 lb	*(450 g)* fusilli
¼ cup	*(60 mL)* olive oil
2 cups	*(500 mL)* tomato purée
1½ tsp	*(8 mL)* dry mustard
1 cup	*(250 mL)* light cream
1 lb	*(450 g)* prosciutto
½ cup	*(125 mL)* grated Parmesan cheese

Cook the noodles al dente in a pot of boiling, salted water.

Heat the oil in a saucepan. Add the tomatoes and mustard; simmer until very thick.

Add the cream and chopped prosciutto. Simmer for 8 minutes.

Pour over noodles. Sprinkle with Parmesan and serve.

Lasagne Seafood Rolls

8 servings

1 lb	(450 g) lasagne noodles
1 cup	(250 mL) baby shrimp
1 cup	(250 mL) cooked, flaked salmon
3/4 cup	(180 mL) grated Parmesan cheese
2	eggs
1 cup	(250 mL) ricotta cheese
1/2 cup	(125 mL) breadcrumbs
1/3 cup	(80 mL) butter
1/3 cup	(80 mL) flour
1 cup	(250 mL) light cream
1 cup	(250 mL) chicken stock (see *Soups*)
1 cup	(250 mL) grated Romano cheese

Preheat oven to 350°F (*180°C*).

Cook the noodles in a large pot until al dente. Rinse under cold water and drain.

Mix the shrimp, salmon, Parmesan, eggs, ricotta and breadcrumbs together.

Lay the noodles flat. Top with filling. Roll up end to end like a jelly roll. Place in a greased casserole dish.

Heat the butter in a saucepan. Add the flour and stir into a roux (paste). Do not brown. Cook 2 minutes.

Add the cream and chicken stock. Simmer until thickened. Pour over noodles. Sprinkle with Romano.

Bake in oven for 30 minutes or until browned.

Cheese Lasagne Verdi

6 servings

1 lb	(450 g) green lasagne noodles
1/4 cup	(60 mL) butter
3/4 lb	(340 g) ricotta cheese
4	eggs
1/2 cup	(125 mL) breadcrumbs
1/2 lb	(225 g) grated mozzarella cheese
1/2 lb	(225 g) grated medium Cheddar
1 tsp	(5 mL) chervil
1 tsp	(5 mL) basil
1 tsp	(5 mL) salt
2 cups	(500 mL) tomato sauce
1 cup	(250 mL) tomato sauce, heated

Preheat oven to 400°F (*200°C*).

Cook the noodles al dente in a large pot of boiling water. Rinse under cold water. Drain.

In a food processor, blend together the butter, ricotta, eggs and breadcrumbs.

Remove and mix in the mozzarella, Cheddar and seasonings.

Grease a large casserole dish. Lay a layer of noodles on the bottom.

Cover with a thin layer of tomato sauce. Top with cheese mixture.

Repeat until all fillings are used, finishing with a layer of cheese mixture.

Bake in oven for 30 minutes or until browned.

Remove and serve with 3 tbsp (*45 mL*) of heated tomato sauce poured over each portion.

Macaroni with Gruyère and Parmesan

8 servings

1 lb	(450 g) elbow macaroni
2 tbsp	(30 mL) butter
1 cup	(250 mL) grated Gruyère cheese
1 cup	(250 mL) grated Parmesan cheese
1/4 cup	(60 mL) heavy cream
1 tsp	(5 mL) salt
1/2 tsp	(3 mL) white pepper

Cook the macaroni al dente in a pot of boiling, salted water. Drain.

While macaroni is still hot, stir in the butter, cheeses, cream and seasonings.

Combine well. Serve.

My Lasagne

10 servings

Sauce

2¼ lbs	*(1 kg)* ground beef
1 lb	*(450 g)* Italian sausage, diced
3	onions, finely diced
1	green pepper, finely diced
4 oz	*(115 g)* mushrooms, sliced
2	celery stalks, finely diced
2 tbsp	*(30 mL)* olive oil
2 cups	*(500 mL)* tomatoes, seeded and chopped
½ cup	*(125 mL)* tomato paste
2 tsp	*(10 mL)* salt
1 tsp	*(5 mL)* pepper
1 tsp	*(5 mL)* garlic powder
1 tsp	*(5 mL)* rosemary
1 tsp	*(5 mL)* oregano
1 tsp	*(5 mL)* basil
1 tsp	*(5 mL)* thyme

1 lb	*(450 g)* lasagne noodles
1 lb	*(450 g)* cottage cheese
1½ lbs	*(675 g)* mozzarella cheese, grated
1 lb	*(450 g)* Cheddar cheese, grated
1 cup	*(250 mL)* grated Parmesan cheese

My Lasagne

Sauce : Brown meats together with vegetables in the oil.

Add tomatoes and tomato paste; simmer 15 minutes.

Add seasonings, reduce heat and simmer for 2 hours.

Cook noodles al dente.

Preheat oven to 350°F *(180°C)*.

Grease a 15 x 10 x 2-in. *(37 x 25 x 5 cm)* casserole or baking dish. Layer noodles, cottage cheese, sauce, grated mozzarella and Cheddar.

Finish so that grated cheese is on top. Sprinkle with Parmesan cheese.

Bake in oven for 45 to 50 minutes.

Remove, slice and serve.

Pasta Stuffed Peppers

6 servings

¾ lb	(*340 g*) macaroni
6	sweet peppers
2 tbsp	(*30 mL*) butter
2 cups	(*500 mL*) tomato sauce
1 tsp	(*5 mL*) basil
2 cups	(*500 mL*) grated mozzarella cheese
½ cup	(*125 mL*) grated Parmesan cheese

Cook the macaroni al dente in a large pot of boiling, salted water. Drain and cool.

Preheat oven to 350°F (*180°C*).

Cut the tops from the peppers. Mince them and sauté them in the butter until tender.

Add the tomato sauce and basil and simmer for 5 minutes.

Mix the sauce with the noodles. Stuff the noodles tightly into the peppers.

Sprinkle with mozzarella and Parmesan. Cover loosely with foil.

Bake in oven for 25 minutes or until the peppers are tender.

Serve at once.

1

Cut the tops from the peppers.

2

Mince tops and sauté in butter. Add the tomato sauce and basil and simmer 5 minutes.

3

Mix sauce with cooked noodles and stuff tightly into peppers. Sprinkle with cheeses.

4

Bake in oven 25 minutes, or until peppers are tender.

Linguine with Prosciutto and Smoked Salmon

8 servings

1 lb	(*450 g*) linguine
2 tbsp	(*30 mL*) butter
1	small onion, finely diced
¼ lb	(*115 g*) prosciutto
⅓ cup	(*80 mL*) sherry
2 cups	(*500 mL*) tomatoes, peeled, seeded and chopped
1 tsp	(*5 mL*) salt
1 tsp	(*5 mL*) paprika
1 tsp	(*5 mL*) basil
½ tsp	(*3 mL*) pepper
¼ lb	(*115 g*) smoked salmon
½ cup	(*125 mL*) heavy cream

Cook the linguine al dente in a large pot of boiling, salted water.

Heat the butter and sauté the onion. Cut the prosciutto into slices. Cook only to heat.

Add the sherry and tomatoes; simmer for 15 minutes. Mash the tomatoes and add the seasonings.

Dice the salmon and add to sauce. Stir in the cream.

Combine the noodles into the sauce and serve at once.

Linguine with Prosciutto and Smoked Salmon

Linguine and Crayfish Diable

6 servings

1 lb	(*450 g*) linguine
3	garlic cloves, minced
1	onion, minced
½ cup	(*125 mL*) olive oil
4	tomatoes, chopped
pinch	sweet basil
½ tsp	(*3 mL*) salt
1 tsp	(*5 mL*) black pepper
2 tsp	(*10 mL*) cayenne pepper
1 tsp	(*5 mL*) chopped parsley
½ cup	(*125 mL*) white wine
1 lb	(*450 g*) crayfish tails, cooked
¼ cup	(*60 mL*) grated Parmesan cheese

Cook linguine al dente.

Sauté garlic and onion in the oil. Add the tomatoes, basil, salt, peppers, parsley and wine.

Simmer 5 minutes, add crayfish and simmer 5 more minutes.

Serve linguine on plates topped with sauce and sprinkle with Parmesan.

Linguine Fisherman-Style

8 servings

¼ cup	(60 mL) olive oil
1	medium onion, finely diced
1	green onion, diced
1	celery stalk, diced
2	garlic cloves, crushed
8 oz	(225 g) shrimp, peeled and deveined
8 oz	(225 g) small scallops
2 cups	(500 mL) tomatoes, seeded and chopped
1 tbsp	(15 mL) basil
1 tbsp	(15 mL) oregano
1 tbsp	(15 mL) parsley
1 tsp	(5 mL) salt
1 tsp	(5 mL) pepper
2¼ lbs	(1 kg) linguine, cooked

Heat the oil in a saucepan. Sauté the vegetables and garlic until tender.

Add the shrimp and scallops and cook 5 minutes.

Add the tomatoes and seasonings and simmer 15 minutes.

Pour sauce over hot linguine. Serve.

Old-Fashioned Macaroni and Cheese

8 servings

1 lb	(450 g) elbow macaroni
3 tbsp	(45 mL) butter
3 tbsp	(45 mL) flour
4 cups	(1 L) heavy cream
pinch	nutmeg
1 tsp	(5 mL) salt
½ tsp	(3 mL) pepper
1 cup	(250 mL) grated sharp Cheddar cheese
2 cups	(500 mL) grated medium Cheddar cheese
1 cup	(250 mL) fine breadcrumbs

Cook the macaroni in boiling water until al dente. Drain and set aside.

Preheat oven to 350°F (180°C).

Heat the butter in a saucepan. Add the flour and stir into a smooth paste (roux); cook for 2 minutes. Do not brown.

Add the cream and stir. Add the seasonings. Reduce heat and simmer to a thick sauce.

Mix the cheeses and add 1½ cups (375 mL) to the sauce.

Butter a casserole dish; sprinkle with half the breadcrumbs.

Add the macaroni. Pour sauce over noodles. Sprinkle with the remaining cheese and breadcrumbs.

Bake in oven until browned. Serve.

Panzerotti

4 servings

3 tbsp	(45 mL) butter
1	small onion, minced
½ cup	(125 mL) minced green peppers
1	celery stalk, minced
2	garlic cloves, crushed
1 cup	(250 mL) chopped cooked chicken
1 cup	(250 mL) tomatoes, seeded and chopped
1 tsp	(5 mL) salt
2 tsp	(10 mL) basil
1 cup	(250 mL) ricotta cheese
1	recipe basic pasta dough
3 cups	(750 mL) oil

Heat the butter in a saucepan.

Add the vegetables and garlic and sauté until tender.

Add the chicken and the tomatoes. Simmer until very thick.

Add the seasonings. Remove from heat and cool. Once cool, blend in the ricotta cheese.

Roll out dough as instructed in basic pasta dough recipe. Cut into 4-in. (10 cm) squares.

Divide the filling among the squares. Fold in half. Seal the edges.

Heat the oil to 350°F (180°C).

Fry the pasta in the oil until golden brown on all sides.

Feta Penne with Veal Tomato Sauce

Feta Penne with Veal Tomato Sauce

8 servings

¼ cup	(60 mL) oil
1½ lbs	(675 g) veal, thinly sliced
2	garlic cloves, minced
1	small onion, minced
1	green pepper, finely diced
2	celery stalks, minced
4 oz	(115 g) mushrooms, sliced
1 tsp	(5 mL) salt
½ tsp	(3 mL) pepper
¼ tsp	(1 mL) oregano
¼ tsp	(1 mL) basil
¼ tsp	(1 mL) thyme
2 cups	(500 mL) crushed tomatoes
½ lb	(225 g) penne noodles
½ cup	(125 mL) crumbled feta cheese

Heat the oil in a large skillet. Brown the veal in the oil. Remove and set aside.

Add the garlic, onion, green pepper, celery and mushrooms; sauté until tender.

Add the seasonings and the tomatoes; reduce heat and simmer for 15 minutes.

Add the veal and simmer for another 10 minutes.

While sauce is simmering, heat 8 cups (2 L) of salted water in a pot to boiling. Add the penne and cook al dente. Drain.

Place the noodles on a serving platter. Top with veal sauce.

Sprinkle with crumbled feta cheese.

Pheasant and Penne

8 servings

3 tbsp	(45 mL) butter
3 tbsp	(45 mL) flour
¼ cup	(60 mL) sherry
1½ cups	(375 mL) heavy cream
1 tsp	(5 mL) salt
¼ tsp	(1 mL) pepper
1 lb	(450 g) pheasant meat, cooked and diced
¼ lb	(115 g) prosciutto, diced
1 lb	(450 g) penne noodles
3 oz	(90 mL) grated Parmesan cheese

Heat the butter in a saucepan. Add the flour and stir into a roux (paste). Do not brown.

Cook roux 2 minutes. Add the sherry and cream. Simmer until sauce thickens.

Add the seasonings, pheasant meat and prosciutto. Simmer another 5 minutes.

Cook noodles al dente in a pot of boiling, salted water. Drain.

Place on a platter. Pour sauce over noodles.

Sprinkle with Parmesan. Serve.

Penne with Four Cheeses

8 servings

½ cup	(125 mL) crumbled ricotta cheese
½ cup	(125 mL) grated Gruyère cheese
½ cup	(125 mL) grated Gouda cheese
½ cup	(125 mL) grated Romano cheese
¼ cup	(60 mL) heavy cream
1 tsp	(5 mL) salt
½ tsp	(3 mL) fresh cracked pepper
2 tsp	(10 mL) parsley flakes
1 lb	(450 g) penne noodles
3 tbsp	(45 mL) butter

Blend the cheeses together. Add the cream, salt and pepper.

Sprinkle in the parsley and combine.

Cook the penne in boiling, salted water until al dente. Drain well.

Blend in the butter and toss in the cheese mixture. Serve at once.

Penne with Smoked Salmon and Snow Peas

4 servings

4 oz	(115 g) snow peas, strings discarded
8 oz	(225 g) penne noodles
¼ cup	(60 mL) butter
¼ cup	(60 mL) flour
1 cup	(250 mL) chicken stock (see *Soups*)
1 cup	(250 mL) heavy cream
3 oz	(90 g) smoked salmon, diced
1 tbsp	(15 mL) parsley flakes
½ cup	(125 mL) grated Romano cheese

Blanch the snow peas for 30 seconds.

In a large pot, boil salted water and cook the penne al dente. Drain and set aside.

In a small saucepan, melt the butter, add the flour and stir into a paste (roux).

Add the chicken stock and cream. Simmer for 10 minutes, stirring occasionally.

Add the salmon and snow peas. Pour sauce over penne.

Sprinkle with parsley. Serve with cheese.

Penne with Smoked Salmon and Snow Peas

Rigatoni alla Vodka

8 servings

1 lb	(*450 g*) rigatoni
2 tbsp	(*30 mL*) butter
1	small onion, minced
1	garlic clove, minced
2 tbsp	(*30 mL*) flour
2 cups	(*500 mL*) light cream
¼ cup	(*60 mL*) vodka
¼ cup	(*60 mL*) tomato paste
1 tsp	(*5 mL*) salt
1 tsp	(*5 mL*) white pepper
1 tsp	(*5 mL*) sweet basil
½ cup	(*125 mL*) grated Romano cheese

In a large pot, boil the rigatoni in salted water.

In a saucepan, melt the butter and add the onion and garlic; sauté until tender.

Add the flour and stir into a smooth paste (roux).

Add the cream, vodka, tomato paste and seasonings. Simmer for 8 minutes.

Toss the noodles in the sauce and serve with Romano.

Rigatoni with Beef, Tomatoes and Mushrooms

8 servings

1 lb	(*450 g*) rigatoni
2 tbsp	(*30 mL*) butter
2 tbsp	(*30 mL*) oil
4 oz	(*115 g*) mushrooms, sliced
½ lb	(*225 g*) beef, thinly sliced
2 cups	(*500 mL*) tomatoes, seeded and chopped
1 tsp	(*5 mL*) salt
1 tsp	(*5 mL*) oregano
1 tsp	(*5 mL*) basil
½ tsp	(*3 mL*) black pepper

In a large pot, cook the rigatoni al dente in boiling, salted water.

Heat the butter with the oil; sauté the mushrooms and the beef until tender.

Add the tomatoes and seasonings. Simmer sauce until thick.

Pour over rigatoni and serve.

Rotini Bolognese

8 servings

¼ lb	(*115 g*) streaky bacon, diced
1	onion, diced
1	celery stalk, diced
1	carrot, diced
1 lb	(*450 g*) lean ground beef
1 lb	(*450 g*) tomatoes, seeded and chopped
6 oz	(*180 mL*) sherry
2 cups	(*500 mL*) beef stock (see *Soups*)
1	bay leaf
2 tsp	(*10 mL*) thyme
2 tsp	(*10 mL*) oregano
2 tsp	(*10 mL*) salt
1 lb	(*450 g*) rotini
¼ cup	(*60 mL*) grated Parmesan cheese

In a large pot, fry the bacon. Add the onion, celery and carrots; sauté until tender.

Add the beef and brown. Add the tomatoes, sherry, stock, and seasonings.

Bring to a boil then reduce heat. Simmer for 1 hour or until sauce is reduced to a nice thickness.

Cook the rotini al dente in a pot of salted water. Drain. Pour into a large bowl.

Smother with sauce. Sprinkle with cheese. Serve.

Ricotta Ravioli

8 servings

3 cups	(*750 mL*) ricotta cheese
2	eggs
½ tsp	(*3 mL*) salt
¼ tsp	(*1 mL*) pepper
½ tsp	(*3 mL*) basil
¾ cup	(*180 mL*) grated Parmesan cheese
1	recipe basic pasta dough

Mix the ricotta with the eggs. Add the seasonings and the Parmesan. Blend thoroughly.

Mix the pasta dough. Roll and cut the dough into strips 6 in. (*15 cm*) wide.

Place 2 tsp (*10 mL*) of ricotta mixture 3 ½ in. (*9 cm*) apart along strips. Fold the dough. over the filling and seal the edges by pressing with a fork .

Cut between each mound of filling, sealing these edges.

Boil a large pot of salted water. Add the ravioli a few at a time. Cook for about 20 minutes.

Serve with your favorite tomato or cheese sauce.

Ricotta Ravioli

Spaghetti Marsala

4 servings

½	recipe basic pasta dough
3 tbsp	(*45 mL*) butter
3 tbsp	(*45 mL*) flour
1 cup	(*250 mL*) heavy cream
½ cup	(*125 mL*) Marsala wine
½ cup	(*125 mL*) grated Parmesan cheese

Roll and cut the dough as instructed in basic pasta dough recipe.

Cut the dough into spaghetti noodles and cook al dente.

Heat the butter in a saucepan.

Add the flour and stir into a roux (paste). Cook 2 minutes.

Add the cream and the wine. Simmer until slightly thickened.

Add the cheese and simmer until thickened.

Pour sauce over noodles. Serve.

Spaghetti Carbonara

8 servings

1 tbsp	(*15 mL*) salt	
1 lb	(*450 g*) spaghetti	
¾ lb	(*340 g*) bacon, diced	
¾ lb	(*340 g*) fresh mushrooms	
6	garlic cloves, minced	
2	onions, finely diced	
¼ cup	(*60 mL*) olive oil	
3	eggs	
¼ cup	(*60 mL*) heavy cream	
1 tbsp	(*15 mL*) cracked black pepper	
½ lb	(*225 g*) grated Parmesan cheese	

Boil water in a large pot; add salt and cook spaghetti.

Sauté the bacon, mushrooms, garlic and onions in the oil until tender. Drain oil.

Mix the eggs, cream, black pepper and Parmesan in a bowl. Stir in the bacon and mushroom mixture.

Drain the spaghetti and toss with the sauce, mixing well. Serve.

Spaghetti, Prosciutto and Gorgonzola

8 servings

1 lb	(*450 g*) spaghetti	
2 tbsp	(*30 mL*) olive oil	
½ lb	(*225 g*) prosciutto, diced	
1½ cups	(*375 mL*) heavy cream	
½ lb	(*225 g*) Gorgonzola cheese	
3 oz	(*90 g*) Romano, grated	

Cook the spaghetti al dente in a large pot of boiling, salted water. Drain.

Heat the oil and add the prosciutto. Cook only to heat.

Add the cream and bring to a simmer. Crumble in the Gorgonzola and stir until sauce thickens.

Pour sauce over noodles. Sprinkle with Romano.

Spaghetti with Pickerel and Herbs

8 servings

1 lb	(*450 g*) spaghetti	
3 tbsp	(*45 mL*) olive oil	
1 lb	(*450 g*) pickerel filets	
3 tbsp	(*45 mL*) butter	
¼ cup	(*60 mL*) flour	
3 cups	(*750 mL*) heavy cream	
½ tsp	(*3 mL*) basil	
½ tsp	(*3 mL*) chervil	
2 tsp	(*10 mL*) chopped parsley	
1 tsp	(*5 mL*) rosemary	
1 tsp	(*5 mL*) salt	
¼ tsp	(*1 mL*) pepper	
1 cup	(*250 mL*) ricotta cheese	
¼ cup	(*60 mL*) grated Parmesan Cheese	

Cook the spaghetti in a large pot of boiling, salted water until al dente. Drain.

Preheat oven to 350°F (*180°C*).

Place noodles in a large greased casserole dish.

Heat the oil in a skillet and sauté the pickerel filets 1½ minutes each side. Lay the filets over the noodles.

Heat the butter in a saucepan, add the flour and stir into a roux (paste). Cook for 2 minutes.

Reduce heat, add the cream and the seasonings. Simmer until sauce thickens slightly.

Add the ricotta and simmer until melted.

Pour sauce over fish and noodles. Sprinkle with Parmesan.

Bake in oven until browned.

Tortellini

8 servings

10 oz	*(280 g)* ricotta cheese
3 oz	*(90 g)* grated Parmesan cheese
2	eggs
1 tbsp	*(15 mL)* chopped parsley
1 tsp	*(5 mL)* oregano
1 tsp	*(5 mL)* thyme
1 tsp	*(5 mL)* basil
1 tsp	*(5 mL)* salt
½ tsp	*(3 mL)* cracked black pepper
1	recipe basic pasta dough

Cream the ricotta in a food processor.

Add the Parmesan and eggs and blend. Add the seasonings and blend.

Roll out the dough as instructed in basic pasta dough recipe.

Cut into circles 1-in. *(2,5 cm)* in diameter. Place 1½ tsp *(8 mL)* of cheese mixture in each circle. Fold circles in half. Seal the edges and shape into tortellini.

Cook by dropping a few at a time in boiling water. Remove as soon as they rise to the surface.

Serve with your choice of tomato, cheese or cream sauce.

1

Roll out dough.

2

Cut into 1-inch *(2,5 cm)* circles and place 1½ tsp *(8 mL)* of cheese mixture in each circle.

3

Fold circles in half, seal the edges and shape into tortellini.

4

Cook by dropping a few at a time in boiling water. Remove as soon as they rise to the surface.

Tortellini Marinara

Tortellini Marinara

10 servings

2¼ lbs	(*1 kg*) tortellini
1½ lbs	(*675 g*) mussels or kiwi clams
1 lb	(*450 g*) medium-size shrimp
1 tbsp	(*30 mL*) oil
1	garlic clove, crushed
3 cups	(*750 mL*) tomatoes, seeded and finely chopped
2 tbsp	(*30 mL*) tomato paste
¼ cup	(*60 mL*) sherry
1½ lbs	(*675 g*) baby scallops
½ cup	(*125 mL*) grated Parmesan cheese

Cook tortellini in rapidly boiling water for 10 minutes or according to directions.

Cook mussels in boiling, salted water until they open. Drain, remove and discard any that do not open.

Remove the flesh and discard the shells. Shell and devein the shrimp.

Heat the oil and sauté the garlic. Add the tomatoes, tomato paste and sherry.

Bring to a boil and reduce heat; simmer for 20 minutes.

Add seafood and continue to simmer an additional 15 minutes.

Serve sauce over tortellini. Sprinkle with Parmesan.

Tortellini Salad

8 servings

½	recipe tortellini
1	onion, diced
1	green pepper, chopped
2	celery stalks, diced
4 oz	(*115 g*) mushrooms, sliced
2 cups	(*500 mL*) chopped tomatoes
1 cup	(*250 mL*) olive oil
⅓ cup	(*80 mL*) vinegar
1 tsp	(*5 mL*) oregano
1 tsp	(*5 mL*) basil
1 tsp	(*5 mL*) thyme
1 tsp	(*5 mL*) salt
½ tsp	(*3 mL*) pepper

Prepare and cook the tortellini according to recipe directions. Drain and cool.

Toss the vegetables and tomatoes together.

Mix the oil with the vinegar and seasonings.

Mix the vegetables with the tortellini. Pour the dressing over the salad.

Tortellini Salad

Tortellini au Gratin

8 servings

¼ lb	(*115 g*) bacon, sliced and diced
3 cups	(*750 mL*) tomato purée
1 tsp	(*5 mL*) chervil
1 tsp	(*5 mL*) thyme
1 tsp	(*5 mL*) oregano
1 tsp	(*5 mL*) salt
1 cup	(*250 mL*) heavy cream
1	recipe tortellini
2 cups	(*500 mL*) grated mozzarella cheese
1 cup	(*250 mL*) grated medium Cheddar

Fry the bacon in a saucepan. Drain excess fat.

Add the tomato purée and seasonings. Simmer and reduce to 2 cups (*500 mL*). Stir in the cream.

Cook the tortellini according to recipe directions. Drain well.

Preheat oven to 350°F (*180°C*).

Place tortellini in a large greased casserole dish.

Pour sauce over tortellini.

Sprinkle with cheeses.

Bake 15 minutes in oven. Serve.

Curried Tortellini and Prawns

6 servings

½ cup	(*125 mL*) butter	
1 lb	(*450 g*) prawns, shelled and deveined	
4 oz	(*115 g*) mushrooms, sliced	
1 tbsp	(*15 mL*) curry powder	
¼ cup	(*60 mL*) flour	
1 cup	(*250 mL*) chicken stock (see *Soups*)	
2 cups	(*500 mL*) heavy cream	
2 tsp	(*10 mL*) salt	
½	recipe tortellini	
2 cups	(*500 mL*) grated mozzarella cheese	

Heat the butter in a saucepan. Sauté the prawns and the mushrooms. Remove and set aside.

Add the curry and flour; stir in a roux (paste). Cook 2 minutes.

Stir in the chicken stock, cream and salt; reduce to a simmer and cook until thickened.

Return the prawns and mushrooms to saucepan.

Cook tortellini according to recipe directions.

Preheat oven to 400°F (*200°C*).

Place tortellini in a large greased casserole dish. Pour sauce over tortellini.

Sprinkle with cheese and brown in oven. Serve.

Tortellini Seafood Soup

8 servings

¼ cup	(*60 mL*) oil	
1	onion, minced	
1	green pepper, minced	
2	celery stalks, minced	
1	garlic clove, minced	
3 cups	(*750 mL*) tomatoes, chopped	
8 cups	(*2 L*) fish stock (see *Soups*)	
1 tsp	(*5 mL*) salt	
1 tbsp	(*15 mL*) chopped parsley	
1 tsp	(*5 mL*) basil	
1 tsp	(*5 mL*) oregano	
1 tsp	(*5 mL*) thyme	
1 tsp	(*5 mL*) paprika	
½ cup	(*125 mL*) Marsala wine	
1 lb	(*450 g*) red snapper, sliced	
1 lb	(*450 g*) shrimp, shelled and deveined	
24	clams	
24	mussels	
½	recipe tortellini, cooked	

In a large pot, heat the oil.

Add onion, green pepper, celery and garlic; sauté until tender.

Add the tomatoes, fish stock, seasonings and wine; bring to boil. Reduce heat and simmer 40 minutes.

Add the red snapper and shrimp; simmer 10 more minutes.

Add the clams and mussels and continue to simmer 5 minutes. Add the tortellini.

Remove from heat; wait 3 minutes and serve.

Seashell Seafood Salad

8 servings

1 lb	(*450 g*) seashell pasta
1	onion, finely diced
1	green pepper, finely diced
1	celery stalk, finely diced
½ lb	(*225 g*) cooked baby shrimp
½ lb	(*225 g*) cooked crab meat
½ lb	(*225 g*) cooked salmon
1 cup	(*250 mL*) mayonnaise
2 tsp	(*10 mL*) basil
1 cup	(*250 mL*) tomatoes, seeded and chopped

Cook the pasta al dente in a pot of boiling, salted water. Rinse under cold water and drain.

Combine the pasta with vegetables and seafood. Mix the mayonnaise, basil and tomatoes together and blend into the pasta. Serve.

Seashell Seafood Salad

Seashell Artichoke Salad

8 servings

1 lb	(*450 g*) seashell pasta
6	artichokes
½ cup	(*125 mL*) olive oil
3 tbsp	(*45 mL*) lemon juice
1 tsp	(*5 mL*) sweet basil
1 tsp	(*5 mL*) salt
½ tsp	(*3 mL*) pepper
1 cup	(*250 mL*) fresh tomatoes, peeled, seeded and chopped

Boil the pasta in salted water until al dente. Drain and rinse under cold water.

Clean, trim and quarter the artichokes.

Remove the core (choke) then boil the quarters in salted water until tender. Drain and cool.

Blend the oil, lemon juice and seasonings together with the tomatoes.

Toss the pasta with the artichokes and pour over the tomato dressing.

Vermicelli Pesto

8 servings

1 lb	(*450 g*) vermicelli
¼ cup	(*60 mL*) basil leaves
3 oz	(*90 g*) Romano cheese, grated
¼ cup	(*60 mL*) chopped parsley
2	garlic cloves
1 tbsp	(*15 mL*) pine nuts
2 tbsp	(*30 mL*) olive oil
2 tbsp	(*30 mL*) beef stock (see *Soups*)

Cook the vermicelli al dente in a large pot. Drain.

Pound the basil, Romano, parsley, garlic and nuts into a smooth paste.

Mix in the oil and beef stock. Pour over noodles.

Vermicelli Edmonton-Style

8 servings

1 lb	(*450 g*) vermicelli
¼ cup	(*60 mL*) olive oil
1	medium onion, finely diced
1	green pepper, finely diced
1	celery stalk, finely diced
2	garlic cloves, crushed
4 cups	(*1 L*) tomatoes, seeded and chopped
1 tbsp	(*15 mL*) basil
1 tbsp	(*15 mL*) oregano
1 tsp	(*5 mL*) black pepper
2 tsp	(*10 mL*) salt
1 lb	(*450 g*) cooked diced chicken
8 oz	(*225 g*) kolbassa (Polish sausage), diced
½ cup	(*125 mL*) grated Parmesan cheese

In a large pot of boiling, salted water, cook the vermicelli al dente.

In a saucepan, heat the oil. Sauté the vegetables and garlic until tender.

Add the tomatoes, seasonings, chicken and kolbassa. Simmer for 20 minutes.

Pour sauce over pasta and serve with cheese.

Vermicelli with Apples

8 servings

2¼ lbs	(*1 kg*) apples, pared, cored and diced
¼ cup	(*60 mL*) oil
1	celery stalk, minced
4 cups	(*1 L*) crushed tomatoes
1 tsp	(*5 mL*) salt
1 tsp	(*5 mL*) basil
¼ tsp	(*1 mL*) cayenne pepper
1 tsp	(*5 mL*) thyme
1 tsp	(*5 mL*) oregano
1 lb	(*450 g*) vermicelli

Purée the apples in a food processor.

Heat the oil in a saucepan. Add the celery and sauté until tender.

Add the tomatoes and seasonings. Simmer for 10 minutes.

Add the puréed apples, reduce heat and simmer for 40 minutes until very thick.

Boil the vermicelli in a pot of salted water until al dente. Drain.

Smother noodles with the sauce and serve.

Breaded Ravioli

8 servings

3 tbsp	(*45 mL*) butter
1½ cups	(*375 mL*) shredded chicken
1 cup	(*250 mL*) ricotta or cream cheese
2	eggs
1 tsp	(*5 mL*) salt
1 tsp	(*5 mL*) basil
½ tsp	(*3 mL*) pepper
1	recipe basic pasta dough
4 cups	(*1 L*) breadcrumbs
2 tsp	(*10 mL*) salt
½ tsp	(*3 mL*) pepper
1 tsp	(*5 mL*) thyme
¼ tsp	(*1 mL*) oregano
3 cups	(*750 mL*) oil

Breaded Ravioli

Heat the butter in a skillet. Sauté the chicken thoroughly. Remove and cool. Once cooled, blend the cheese and chicken together.

Add the eggs and seasonings.

Prepare the dough as instructed in basic pasta dough recipe. Cut and roll out.

Cut the dough into strips 5 in. (*12 cm*) wide. Place 2 tsp (*10 mL*) of filling 3 ½ in. (*9 cm*) apart along strips.

Fold the dough over the filling and seal the edges by pressing with a fork.

Cut between the mounds and seal the edges.

Blend the breadcrumbs with the seasonings.

Roll each ravioli in the seasoned breadcrumbs.

Heat the oil to 350°F (*180°C*); deep fry a few ravioli at a time.

Cook for about 2½ minutes. Serve with tomato sauce.

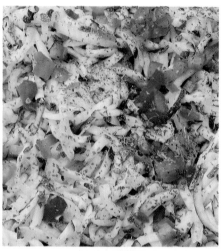

Vegetables

"Eat up your vegetables" is a constant refrain in many households. The sad truth is that the vegetables served in many homes and restaurants are not worth eating. Why is it that so many people treat vegetables as an after-thought, or boil the life out of them until they are nothing but mush?

Vegetables properly cooked are a pleasure to look at and a real delight to the taste buds. And really good cooks know that vegetables add more than vitamins and minerals to a meal. They are an important source of color and texture, adding infinitely to the overall aesthetic pleasure of the dining experience.

When you plan a meal, think of the vegetables as part of the "total package". Consider the following points :

Color : No matter how good the ingredients, no meal is interesting unless it has visual appeal. Since vegetables come in such a wide choice of colors, they are an easy way to liven up a boring plate.

Flavor : Always choose vegetables at their peak of freshness. New, small or "baby" vegetables have the finest flavor.

Shape : Select vegetables that will provide variation in shape. A plate of meatballs would look quite silly served with cherry tomatoes and small whole potatoes. Add variation by using different shapes — dice, sticks, ovals and rings.

Texture : Again, variety is the catchword. A meal in which everything is mashed or puréed is tedious. Texture adds excitement.

Tips For Cooking Vegetables

When boiling vegetables, use only enough salted water to cover them. Do not try to cook large quantities at a time.

If you use frozen vegetables, thaw them first, and cut down on the recommended cooking time.

Broccoli in Puff Pastry

Broccoli in Puff Pastry

8 servings

1½ cups	(375 mL) sliced mushrooms
2 tbsp	(30 mL) butter
2 cups	(500 mL) chopped broccoli
14 oz	(398 g) pkg. frozen puff pastry, thawed
1 cup	(250 mL) grated Swiss cheese
1	egg, beaten
2 tbsp	(30 mL) milk

Preheat oven to 425°F (220°C).

Sauté mushrooms in butter over high heat until tender, about 3 minutes; set aside.

Cook broccoli in boiling, salted water until almost tender; drain and set aside.

Roll puff pastry into a 16 x 8-in. (40 x 20 cm) rectangle.

Cut into eight 4-in. (10 cm) squares.

Place some of the mushrooms, broccoli, and cheese on each square.

Moisten the edges with water, and fold diagonally; pinch pastry edges to seal.

Combine egg and milk; brush over turnovers.

Bake in oven 12 to 15 minutes or until golden brown.

Asparagus Shrimp Béarnaise

4 servings

1	bunch asparagus
4 cups	(*1 L*) water
2 tsp	(*10 mL*) salt
1 cup	(*250 mL*) baby shrimp, minced
1 cup	(*250 mL*) Béarnaise Sauce (see *Sauces*)

Cook the asparagus in the water and salt until tender. Drain well.

Place on a heat-proof serving platter. Sprinkle with shrimp.

Pour sauce over asparagus.

Place under a broiler for 30 seconds. Serve.

Asparagus Casserole

8 servings

2¼ lbs	(*1 kg*) fresh asparagus, cut into 1-in. (*2,5 cm*) pieces
10 oz	(*284 mL*) can condensed cream of mushroom soup
2 cups	(*500 mL*) crushed plain crackers
½ cup	(*125 mL*) melted butter
2 cups	(*500 mL*) grated old Cheddar cheese
1 cup	(*250 mL*) cashews

Preheat oven to 350°F (*180°C*).

Cook asparagus in boiling, salted water, covered, until almost tender, about 3 to 5 minutes.

Drain, reserving 1¼ cups (*310 mL*) cooking liquid.

Combine mushroom soup with reserved cooking liquid; blend until smooth.

Combine crushed crackers, butter, and cheese; mix well.

Sprinkle half the crumb mixture into a 13 x 9 in. (*33 x 23 cm*) greased baking dish.

Top with half the asparagus, half the nuts, and half the mushroom soup mixture.

Repeat layers.

Bake in oven 30 to 40 minutes.

Artichokes au Gratin

6 servings

6	artichokes
2 cups	(*500 mL*) Mornay Sauce (see *Sauces*)
1 tsp	(*5 mL*) salt
¼ tsp	(*1 mL*) pepper
½ cup	(*125 mL*) grated Parmesan cheese
2 tbsp	(*30 mL*) butter

Preheat oven to 375°F (*190°C*).

Remove the outer leaves and bottoms of the artichokes.

Parboil in salted water until tender. Arrange in a casserole dish.

Pour sauce over artichokes. Season with salt and pepper. Sprinkle with cheese.

Dot with butter.

Bake in oven until cheese melts.

Asparagus Shrimp Béarnaise and Artichokes au Gratin

Broccoli Surprise

Broccoli and Cauliflower in Orange Almond Sauce

8 servings

¾ lb	(*340 g*) broccoli florets
¾ lb	(*340 g*) cauliflower florets
2 tbsp	(*30 mL*) butter
2 tbsp	(*30 mL*) flour
1¼ cups	(*310 mL*) orange juice
¼ cup	(*60 mL*) brown sugar
⅓ cup	(*80 mL*) toasted slivered almonds

Cook the broccoli and cauliflower in boiling, salted water until tender.

Heat the butter in a saucepan. Stir in the flour and cook for 2 minutes.

Stir in the orange juice and sugar. Simmer until thick. Stir in the almonds.

Place vegetables in a serving bowl.

Pour sauce over vegetables and serve.

Broccoli Surprise

6 servings

2 cups	(*500 mL*) cooked broccoli
1½ cups	(*375 mL*) heavy cream
1 cup	(*250 mL*) grated Havarti cheese
4	eggs, beaten

Preheat oven to 350°F (*180°C*).

In a food processor, purée the broccoli. Add the cream and cheese. Process 30 seconds. Add the eggs; process another 30 seconds.

Generously grease a muffin tin. Pour mixture into muffin cups.

Place in a hot water bath and bake in over for 40 to 45 minutes.

Remove, turn out and serve.

Brussels Sprouts Paprika

6 servings

1½ lbs	(675 g) Brussels sprouts
4 cups	(1 L) chicken broth
¼ cup	(60 mL) butter
¼ cup	(60 mL) flour
1 cup	(250 mL) milk
1 tsp	(5 mL) salt
¼ tsp	(1 mL) white pepper
2 tsp	(10 mL) paprika

Wash and trim the Brussels sprouts.

Heat the chicken broth. Cook the sprouts in 3 cups (750 mL) chicken broth. Drain and keep hot.

Heat the butter in a saucepan. Stir in the flour. Cook for 2 minutes.

Stir in the remaining broth and the milk.

Add seasonings. Simmer until thick.

Pour over sprouts and serve.

Brussels Sprouts Bonne Femme

Brussels Sprouts Bonne Femme

4 servings

1 lb	(450 g) Brussels sprouts
4 oz	(115 g) bacon
1 tbsp	(15 mL) flour
1 cup	(250 mL) chicken broth
½ cup	(125 mL) finely diced onions

Trim the sprouts. Blanch 10 to 12 minutes in boiling, salted water.

Dice the bacon. Fry until tender. Drain all but 1 tbsp (15 mL) of grease.

Sprinkle with flour and cook 2 minutes. Add the broth, onions and the sprouts.

Reduce heat and simmer gently until thickened.

Serve hot.

Just Peachy Carrots

4 servings

1 lb	(*450 g*) frozen baby carrots
1½ cups	(*375 mL*) apple juice
3 tbsp	(*45 mL*) butter
2 tbsp	(*30 mL*) brown sugar
3	peaches, peeled and sliced

In a saucepan, cook the carrots in the apple juice until tender. Drain.

Heat the butter in a skillet. Add the brown sugar, stir until sugar melts.

Sauté the peach slices until tender. Add the carrots.

Toss only to glaze. Serve.

Baked Carrots and Apples

4 servings

6	carrots, thinly sliced
1	apple, peeled, cored and sliced
1 tsp	(*5 mL*) grated lemon rind
½ tbsp	(*8 mL*) softened butter
3 tbsp	(*45 mL*) water
	salt and pepper
½ cup	(*125 mL*) grated old Cheddar cheese

Preheat oven to 400°F (*200°C*).

Combine sliced carrots and apples with the lemon rind in a 3-cup (*750 mL*) greased baking dish.

Top with butter, drizzle with water, sprinkle with salt and pepper.

Cover and bake in oven for 20 to 25 minutes or until carrots are tender.

Remove cover, drain, and sprinkle with cheese.

Serve as soon as cheese melts.

Julienned Carrots with Cheddar Sauce

6 servings

1 lb	(*450 g*) carrots, cut in julienne
3 tbsp	(*45 mL*) butter
3 tbsp	(*45 mL*) flour
¾ cup	(*180 mL*) chicken broth
½ cup	(*125 mL*) heavy cream
1 cup	(*250 mL*) grated medium Cheddar
1 tsp	(*5 mL*) salt
¼ tsp	(*1 mL*) white pepper

Boil the carrots in salted water until tender.

Place in a serving bowl and keep hot.

Heat the butter in a saucepan. Stir in the flour. Cook for 2 minutes.

Add the broth and cream. Simmer 8 minutes.

Stir in the cheese and seasonings; simmer 4 more minutes.

Pour sauce over carrots. Serve hot.

Cashew Carrots

8 servings

8	medium carrots, cut in julienne
¾ cup	(*180 mL*) orange juice
¼ cup	(*60 mL*) melted butter
2 tsp	(*10 mL*) honey
½ tsp	(*3 mL*) salt
¼ tsp	(*1 mL*) white pepper
1 tbsp	(*15 mL*) lemon juice
¼ tsp	(*1 mL*) lemon zest
½ cup	(*125 mL*) cashews, coarsely chopped

Cook the carrots in the orange juice until tender. Drain.

Melt the butter in a skillet.

Add the honey, salt, pepper, lemon juice and lemon zest.

Add the carrots and toss to coat.

Add the cashews and serve.

Cashew Carrots

Ratatouille

8 servings

¼ cup	(*60 mL*) olive oil
2	onions, diced
2	garlic cloves, minced
2	medium eggplants, diced
3	zucchini, sliced
2	green peppers, sliced
3 cups	(*750 mL*) tomatoes, seeded and chopped
1 tsp	(*5 mL*) basil
1 tsp	(*5 mL*) chervil
1 tsp	(*5 mL*) salt
2 tsp	(*10 mL*) chopped parsley

Preheat oven to 350°F (*180°C*).

Heat the oil in a saucepan.

Add the vegetables, tomatoes and seasonings. Stir well.

Place in a casserole dish. Cover and bake in oven 40 to 45 minutes.

Serve either hot or cold.

1

In a saucepan, sauté the vegetables in the oil.

2

Add tomatoes and seasonings. Stir well.

3

Place mixture in a casserole dish and bake in oven 40 to 45 minutes.

4

Serve either hot or cold.

Tomatoes Provençale

Tomatoes Provençale

4 servings

4	tomatoes
1 tbsp	(*15 mL*) olive oil
2 tbsp	(*30 mL*) butter
1	garlic clove, minced
2 tbsp	(*30 mL*) minced onion
¼ tsp	(*1 mL*) salt
¼ tsp	(*1 mL*) pepper
½ tsp	(*3 mL*) chervil
1 tbsp	(*15 mL*) chopped parsley
⅓ cup	(*80 mL*) grated Parmesan cheese

Slice the tomatoes in half. Seed and scoop out the pulp; reserve.

Heat the oil in a skillet. Place tomatoes, cut side into the oil.

Cook until the sides are caramelized. Remove and place on a pastry sheet.

Add the butter to the skillet. Add the garlic and onion. Sauté until tender.

Stir in the seasonings and tomato pulp.

Sauté for 1 minute. Fill the tomato cavities with mixture.

Sprinkle with cheese. Place under broiler until browned, about 2 minutes.

Serve hot or cold.

Zucchini Provençale

6 servings

3 tbsp	(*45 mL*) butter
3	zucchini, cut in julienne
2	garlic cloves, minced
1	onion, sliced
3 cups	(*750 mL*) tomatoes, seeded and chopped
1 tsp	(*5 mL*) salt
¼ tsp	(*1 mL*) pepper
1 tsp	(*5 mL*) chervil
½ tsp	(*3 mL*) basil
½ cup	(*125 mL*) sweet white wine

Heat the butter in a large skillet.

Sauté the zucchini, garlic and onion until tender.

Add the tomatoes, seasonings and wine. Reduce heat.

Simmer slowly until liquid is completely reduced.

Serve as a side dish, or over rice.

Zucchini Provençale

Cinnamon Spaghetti Squash

8 servings

1	spaghetti squash
¾ cup	(*180 mL*) brown sugar
1 tsp	(*5 mL*) ground cinnamon
¼ cup	(*60 mL*) butter

Bake the squash whole in a 350°F (*180°C*) oven for 1¼ hours.

With a fork, grate out pulp of squash. Place the squash in a lightly buttered casserole dish.

Sprinkle with sugar and cinnamon. Dot with butter.

Return to oven for 15 more minutes. Serve very hot.

Potato Broccoli Casserole

6 servings

1½ lbs	(*675 g*) potatoes
¼ cup	(*60 mL*) butter
3 tbsp	(*45 mL*) flour
2½ cups	(*625 mL*) milk
½ tsp	(*3 mL*) salt
¼ tsp	(*1 mL*) pepper
1 lb	(*450 g*) broccoli
½ cup	(*125 mL*) grated Parmesan cheese

Preheat oven to 350°F (*180°C*).

Wash and pare the potatoes. Cut into very thin slices.

Heat the butter in a saucepan. Sprinkle with flour, cook for 2 minutes.

Add the milk and seasonings. Simmer until boiling. Remove from heat.

In a large greased casserole dish, layer the potatoes, alternating with sauce and broccoli pieces.

Finish with a top layer of sauce. Sprinkle with Parmesan.

Bake, covered, for 15 minutes and continue to bake for an additional 5 minutes, uncovered.

Remove from oven. Cool for 5 minutes. Serve.

Potato Broccoli Casserole

Creamed Potatoes with Peas

4 servings

4	large potatoes
1½ cups	(*375 mL*) heavy cream
1 cup	(*250 mL*) peas, fresh or frozen
1 tsp	(*5 mL*) salt
¼ tsp	(*1 mL*) pepper

Pare and slice the potatoes. Parboil 10 minutes.

Bring the cream to a boil.

Place the potatoes in a saucepan. Add the peas and seasonings.

Pour in the cream and simmer until the cream is reduced by half.

Potatoes should thicken the cream.

Chantilly Potatoes

6 servings

1 cup	(*250 mL*) heavy cream
1 cup	(*250 mL*) grated Havarti cheese
2 tsp	(*10 mL*) salt
4 cups	(*1 L*) mashed potatoes, hot

Preheat oven to 400°F (*200°C*).

Whip the cream until stiff. Fold in the cheese and salt.

Place the mashed potatoes in a casserole dish.

Spread the cream over the potatoes.

Bake, uncovered, in oven 15 to 20 minutes, or until golden brown.

Maitre d'Hôtel Potatoes

4 servings

6	medium potatoes
2 cups	(*500 mL*) milk
½ tsp	(*3 mL*) salt
¼ tsp	(*1 mL*) white pepper
2 tbsp	(*30 mL*) chopped parsley
1 tsp	(*5 mL*) basil

Parboil the potatoes for 10 minutes in boiling, salted water. Drain.

Peel and slice the potatoes into ¼-in. (*1 cm*) thick slices. Place in a large saucepan.

Heat the milk to a boil. Pour over the potatoes.

Simmer, reducing the milk until the sauce thickens.

Sprinkle with seasonings.

Place in a serving bowl. Serve at once.

Chantilly Potatoes and Maitre d'Hôtel Potatoes

Chive Potato Pancakes

8 servings

Pancakes

2	eggs
3	medium potatoes, pared and shredded
2 tbsp	(*30 mL*) flour
⅓ cup	(*80 mL*) minced chives
¼ tsp	(*1 mL*) pepper
½ tsp	(*3 mL*) salt
	oil for frying

Sauce

2 cups	(*500 mL*) sour cream
1 cup	(*250 mL*) bacon, cooked and crumbled
½ cup	(*125 mL*) minced chives

In a mixing bowl, blend the eggs, potatoes and flour together.

Add the chives and seasonings. Combine well.

Heat a little oil in a large skillet. Drop the batter into the hot oil by tablespoons.

Fry each side crisp and brown. Serve with sauce.

To make sauce, blend the ingredients together well.

Chive Potato Pancakes

Potato Nests

6 servings

8	medium potatoes
4 cups	(*1 L*) oil

Pare and shred the potatoes. Place some of the potatoes in a small sieve or basket.

Press a second sieve or basket into the first, forcing the potatoes to hollow in the center.

Heat the oil to 375°F (*190°C*).

Fry the potatoes in the baskets until golden brown.

Remove the smaller sieve. Turn out the remaining baskets or nests when cooked.

Fill with your choice of accompaniment to the main course.

Timothy's Tummy Tickler

Timothy's Tummy Tickler

	6 servings

6	baked potatoes, chilled
	vegetable oil
	seasoned salt
¾ cup	(*180 mL*) grated medium Cheddar cheese
¾ cup	(*180 mL*) grated Havarti cheese
4	slices bacon, cooked and crumbled

½ cup (*125 mL*) sour cream

Cut the potatoes in wedges and fry without crowding in ¾ in. (*2 cm*) hot oil, until golden.

Place the potatoes on a baking sheet, sprinkle lightly with seasoned salt, the grated cheeses, and the crumbled bacon.

Place under the broiler until the cheese melts.

Serve hot with sour cream on the side.

Desserts

Almost everyone has some kind of sweet tooth, although some of us are addicted to chocolate, others to ice cream, and many have a passion for anything that involves fruit.

Fortunately, this chapter has a dessert to thrill every sweet tooth of your acquaintance. Many of them are "old favorites", and are sure to become "new favorites" to young people who have never tasted them.

For example, you will find recipes for such classics as "Old-Fashioned Apple Pie" and "New York Style Cheesecake". And you can even try your hand at homemade ice cream.

You will notice that a good number of the recipes in this chapter are based on chocolate.

First used by the Aztecs, chocolate was introduced to Europe by the Spanish conquistadors. In its history, it has been known not just as a food, but as a stimulant, aphrodisiac, currency and sacred substance.

The Dutch refined the cacao beans into a powder and discovered the wonders of cocoa butter, which was soon made into the revered chocolate bar. It was back in North America where chocolate finally came into its own as the foundation for numerous fortunes — the Hersheys, Cadburys, Mars and Frys.

Try some of these chocolate recipes and become part of a great tradition.

Pies, Cakes and Cookies

Nothing is quite as rewarding as the smiles and praise you receive when you present your friends or family with a home-baked pie or cake. It makes your work in the kitchen truly a "labor of love".

Unfortunately, many home cooks today seem to have lost the art of baking for their loved ones, which is a shame. We hope you will abandon any reservations you may have about baking and try some of the recipes in this section.

Just remember that the art of baking is a precise one, so you have to follow some simple rules.

1. Always read your recipe through before you begin.

2. Prepare and grease all your pans in advance. Get out all your ingredients and have them at room temperature.

3. Preheat your oven in plenty of time. You should check your oven every year to make sure it is baking at the selected temperature.

4. Follow mixing instructions exactly. Sift all dry ingredients together to make sure they are well mixed.

5. Whip egg whites to stiff peaks before folding them into batters. Do not overmix.

6. Overmixing is the major reason for tough pie crusts. When you cut the butter or shortening into the flour, cut only until a very coarse meal texture. This will produce a far flakier crust. To add to the flakiness, mix an egg or a little vinegar into your dough.

Cooking with Fruit

Fresh fruit provides incomparable flavor, but must be handled carefully.

To prevent fruit from turning brown (caused when the enzymes oxidize tannins in the fruit), brush the fruit with something acidic, such as lemon juice. Or add an antioxidant, such as sugar or salt.

Chocolate Pralines

12-16 pieces

1½ cups	(*375 mL*) dark brown sugar, firmly packed
¾ cup	(*180 mL*) heavy cream
¼ cup	(*60 mL*) butter
4 oz	(*115 g*) semi-sweet chocolate
1 cup	(*250 mL*) pecan pieces

In a heavy saucepan, combine the sugar and cream.

Stirring constantly, heat to 240°F (*115°C*) on a candy thermometer.

Remove from heat, stir in the butter and chocolate. Cool to 110°F (*43°C*).

Stir in the pecans.

Drop spoonfuls of mixture onto a lightly greased pastry sheet.

Allow to cool and harden.

Chocolate Pound Cake

8-10 servings

½ cup	(*125 mL*) butter
1 cup	(*250 mL*) shortening
2 cups	(*500 mL*) sugar
6	eggs
1 tbsp	(*15 mL*) vanilla
1 tbsp	(*15 mL*) orange juice
1 tbsp	(*15 mL*) lemon juice
2 cups	(*500 mL*) flour
1 cup	(*250 mL*) apricot jam
10 oz	(*280 g*) semi-sweet chocolate
2 tbsp	(*30 mL*) melted butter

Preheat oven to 325°F (*160°C*).

Cream the butter, shortening and sugar until light and fluffy.

Beat in eggs, one at a time. Add vanilla, juices and flour.

Combine only until incorporated.

Pour into a lightly greased 11 x 7-in. (*28 x 18 cm*) loaf pan.

Bake in oven 55 to 60 minutes. Remove; cool 5 minutes.

Unmold. Place on a cooling rack.

Heat the jam in a small saucepan. Purée into a smooth paste.

Melt the chocolate and melted butter together in a double boiler.

Brush the cooled cake with the jam. Pour the chocolate over the cake.

Refrigerate until hardened.

Chocolate Pie

8 servings

1½ cups	(*375 mL*) chocolate wafers, crushed fine
¼ cup	(*60 mL*) sugar
6 tbsp	(*90 mL*) melted butter
5 oz	(*150 g*) semi-sweet chocolate
¼ cup	(*60 mL*) heavy cream
4	eggs, separated and at room temperature
1 tsp	(*5 mL*) vanilla extract

Preheat oven to 350°F (*180°C*).

Mix the wafers with 2 tbsp (*30 mL*) sugar and the melted butter.

Press into a 9-in. (*22-cm*) pie plate. Bake in the center rack of oven for 6 minutes. Remove and cool.

In a double boiler, melt the chocolate with the cream.

Add the remaining sugar and stir until smooth. Let cool.

Once cooled, fold in 1 egg yolk at a time, incorporating thoroughly before adding the next. Add the vanilla.

Whip the egg whites until stiff. Gently fold the chocolate mixture into the egg whites.

Pour into cooled pie shell. Refrigerate for 4 hours.

Chocolate Pie

Chocolate Orange Cake

8-10 servings

4 oz	(*115 g*) semi-sweet chocolate
1 tbsp	(*15 mL*) cocoa powder
2 tbsp	(*30 mL*) baking powder
2 cups	(*500 mL*) sifted pastry flour
½ cup	(*125 mL*) butter
1 cup	(*250 mL*) sugar
⅔ cup	(*160 mL*) orange juice
3	egg whites, whipped stiff

Preheat oven to 350°F (*180°C*).

In a double boiler, melt the chocolate.

In a bowl, sift together the cocoa powder, baking powder and flour.

In another bowl, cream the butter with the sugar until very light.

Add the dry ingredients and the orange juice, alternating ⅓ of each at a time.

Blend in the melted chocolate. Fold in the egg whites. Lightly grease and flour two 9-in. (*22 cm*) cake pans.

Bake in oven 20 to 25 minutes. Cool 5 minutes. Turn out on racks.

Frost or ice with chocolate icing.

Chocolate Mousse

Chocolate Mousse

4 servings

1⅓ cups	(*330 mL*) semi-sweet chocolate
⅓ cup	(*80 mL*) black coffee
1 tbsp	(*15 mL*) butter
2 tbsp	(*30 mL*) Triple Sec liqueur
4	eggs
1¼ cups	(*310 mL*) whipping cream

Melt the chocolate in a double boiler. Add the coffee. Remove from heat, stir in the butter and Triple Sec.

Separate the eggs. Add the yolks one at a time, blending them into the warm chocolate.

Whip the egg whites until stiff and fold into the chocolate mixture.

Pour into dessert glasses.

Whip the cream and pipe on top of each serving.

Nanaimo Bars

12-16 bars

Prepare first layer, the cookie crust, and press into a pan.

Layer # 1

½ cup	(125 mL) butter
¼ cup	(60 mL) sugar
¼ cup	(60 mL) cocoa powder
1	egg, beaten
1½ cups	(375 mL) graham cracker crumbs
1 cup	(250 mL) coconut
½ cup	(125 mL) walnuts

In a double boiler, melt the butter, sugar and cocoa powder. Fold in the egg. Stir until thickened, then remove at once from heat. Fold in the remaining ingredients. Press into a 9 x 9 in. (22 X 22 cm) pan.

Pour pudding layer on top of cookie crust.

Layer # 2

½ cup	(125 mL) butter
3 tbsp	(45 mL) heavy cream
2 tbsp	(30 mL) vanilla pudding mix
2 cups	(500 mL) icing sugar

Cream together the butter, cream and pudding mix. Fold in the sugar. Beat until very light. Pour on top of the cookie crust.

Melt chocolate in double boiler, cool and spread on top of second layer.

Layer # 3

1 cup	(250 mL) semi-sweet chocolate
1 tbsp	(15 mL) butter

In a double boiler, melt the chocolate. Fold in the butter. Cool. Pour onto second layer. Refrigerate for 2 hours. Cut and serve.

Refrigerate for 2 hours, then cut and serve.

Apple Pecan Pudding

8 servings

1 cup	(250 mL)	flour
1 tsp	(5 mL)	baking powder
1 tsp	(5 mL)	cinnamon
¼ tsp	(1 mL)	allspice
¼ tsp	(1 mL)	mace
¼ tsp	(1 mL)	salt
¼ cup	(60 mL)	softened butter
1 cup	(250 mL)	sugar
1		egg
2 cups	(500 mL)	apples, pared and diced
½ cup	(125 mL)	pecan pieces

Preheat oven to 350°F (180°C).

Sift together the flour, baking powder, cinnamon, allspice, mace and salt.

In a large bowl, cream the butter with the sugar.

Add the egg. Slowly blend in the flour. Stir in apples and pecans.

Pour into a lightly greased 9-in. (22 cm) cake pan.

Bake in oven 40 to 45 minutes.

Serve with a hot Raspberry Coulis (see *Sauces*).

Apple Fritters

8 servings

1 cup	(250 mL)	flour
2 tsp	(10 mL)	baking powder
1 tsp	(5 mL)	salt
¼ cup	(60 mL)	sugar
¼ tsp	(1 mL)	cinnamon
½ cup	(125 mL)	milk
1		egg
2 tsp	(10 mL)	vanilla extract
1 tbsp	(15 mL)	melted butter
1 cup	(250 mL)	diced apples
4 cups	(1 L)	oil
¼ cup	(60 mL)	cinnamon sugar*

Sift together the flour, baking powder, salt, sugar and cinnamon.

Combine together the milk, egg, vanilla and butter. Blend into the flour mixture. Mix in the apples.

Heat the oil to 375°F (190°C). Drop spoonfuls of fritter batter into oil.

Fry to golden brown on all sides. Place on draining tray. Sprinkle with cinnamon sugar while hot.

*To make cinnamon sugar, mix ¼ cup (60 mL) sugar with 2 tsp (10 mL) cinnamon.

Apple Flan

8 servings

1 cup	(250 mL)	sifted flour
½ cup	(125 mL)	softened butter
1 tbsp	(15 mL)	sugar
½ tsp	(3 mL)	grated lemon rind
pinch		salt
1		egg yolk
1 tbsp	(15 mL)	ice water
1 cup	(250 mL)	sugar
1 tsp	(5 mL)	cinnamon
4 cups	(1 L)	apples, peeled and sliced
½ cup	(125 mL)	melted butter

Sift flour into mixing bowl. Cut in the softened butter. Add 1 tbsp (15 mL) sugar, lemon rind, salt and egg yolk.

Mix the ingredients into a paste, using only as much water as needed.

Work dough into a ball. Wrap dough and chill one hour.

Roll out dough onto a floured surface. Roll out about 2 in. (5 cm) larger than a flan pan.

Put dough in pan. Press into the sides and bottom. Refrigerate 2 hours before using.

Preheat oven to 400°F (200°C).

Mix 1 cup (250 mL) sugar with the cinnamon. Sprinkle on apples. Pour melted butter over and mix.

Place apples in prepared flan dish. Bake in oven 40 minutes.

Apple Pizza Pie

Apple Pizza Pie

8 servings

½	recipe pizza dough
6 cups	(*1,5 L*) sliced apples
2 tbsp	(*30 mL*) lemon juice
½ cup	(*125 mL*) brown sugar
1¼ tsp	(*6 mL*) cinnamon
¼ cup	(*60 mL*) butter
½ cup	(*125 mL*) breadcrumbs
1 cup	(*250 mL*) grated Cheddar cheese
1 cup	(*250 mL*) grated mozzarella cheese

Preheat oven to 450°F (*230°C*).

Make the pizza dough according to recipe directions.

Sprinkle the apples with the lemon juice.

Roll out the dough into a 15-in. (*37 cm*) circle and place on a greased pastry sheet, or on a pizza pan.

Place the apples on the dough. Sprinkle with sugar and cinnamon.

Cut the butter into the breadcrumbs. Sprinkle onto the apples.

Sprinkle with cheeses.

Bake in oven 20 minutes, or until golden brown. Serve hot.

Banana Fritters

8 servings

2	eggs
3 tbsp	(*45 mL*) sugar
½ tsp	(*3 mL*) baking powder
¾ cup	(*180 mL*) flour
4	ripe bananas, mashed
2 cups	(*500 mL*) oil
1 tsp	(*5 mL*) cinnamon
3 tbsp	(*45 mL*) sugar

Beat the eggs.

Sift together 3 tbsp (*45 mL*) sugar, baking powder and flour. Blend into the eggs. Stir in the bananas. Mix thoroughly.

Heat the oil to 350°F (*180°C*). Drop spoonfuls of batter into oil. Cook until golden brown.

Mix the cinnamon with 3 tbsp (*45 mL*) sugar and sprinkle on fritters.

Peach and Pear Salad

6 servings

6	clingstone peaches
6	red Bartlett pears
2 tbsp	(*30 mL*) lemon juice
¾ cup	(*180 mL*) sugar
2 cups	(*500 mL*) water
½ tsp	(*3 mL*) cinnamon
½ cup	(*125 mL*) red currant jelly
6	romaine lettuce leaves

Peel and slice the peaches. Core and slice the pears. Place peaches and pears in a bowl. Sprinkle with lemon juice. Chill.

In a saucepan, dissolve the sugar in water, add the cinnamon and jelly. Bring to a boil, reduce heat and simmer until reduced to ⅓. Cool.

Pour sauce over fruit. Arrange fruit on lettuce leaves and serve.

Cherries Jubilee

6 servings

2	10 oz (*284 mL*) cans cherries
¼ cup	(*60 mL*) cherry brandy
2 tbsp	(*30 mL*) cornstarch
	vanilla ice cream

Drain the cherries. Reserve the liquid. Heat the cherries in a saucepan. Flame with the cherry brandy.

Mix the cornstarch in 1½ cups (*375 mL*) of the reserved liquid. Add to cherries. Simmer until thickened.

Divide into 6 portions and spoon the cherries and juice over 1 scoop of ice cream for each serving. Serve at once.

Cherries Jubilee and Peach and Pear Salad

Chocolate Ice Cream

6 cups (1,5 L)

1 cup	(250 mL) sugar
pinch	salt
1 tbsp	(15 mL) cocoa powder
¼ cup	(60 mL) water
2 oz	(60 g) unsweetened chocolate
4 cups	(1 L) half & half cream
1 tsp	(5 mL) vanilla extract

Dissolve the sugar, salt and cocoa powder in the water. Add the chocolate and melt in a double boiler. Slowly add the half & half and heat. Remove from heat and cool. Add vanilla and freeze according to directions of ice cream maker.

Rocky Road Ice Cream

6 cups (1,5 L)

1	recipe chocolate ice cream
⅓ cup	(80 mL) chopped walnuts
⅓ cup	(80 mL) chocolate chips
⅓ cup	(80 mL) miniature marshmallows

When chocolate ice cream is half frozen in ice cream maker, fold in the walnuts, chocolate chips and marshmallows, then finish freezing.

Rocky Road Ice Cream

Vanilla Ice Cream

4 cups (1 L)

2 cups	(500 mL) light cream or half & half
½ cup	(125 mL) fine sugar
pinch	salt
4	egg yolks
2 tsp	(10 mL) vanilla
1 cup	(250 mL) whipping cream

Combine the light cream, sugar, salt, egg yolks and vanilla.

Cook in a double boiler 25 to 30 minutes, or until very thick. Cool.

Stir in the whipping cream and freeze according to directions of ice cream maker.

Almond Torte

two 9-in. (22 cm) tortes

Pastry

2 cups	(500 mL) pastry flour
2 tsp	(10 mL) baking powder
¼ tsp	(1 mL) salt
½ cup	(125 mL) sugar
1 cup	(250 mL) butter
1	egg
1 tsp	(5 mL) grated lemon rind

Filling

4 cups	(1 L) finely ground almonds
4 cups	(1 L) confectioners' sugar
2	egg whites
½ cup	(125 mL) Amaretto liqueur
⅔ cup	(160 mL) raspberry preserves

Pastry : Sift together the dry ingredients into a mixing bowl. Cut in the butter and mix into a coarse meal.

Whip the egg together with the lemon rind. Stir into pastry.

Divide into two equal portions. Roll out on a lightly flour-dusted surface into two 12-in. (30 cm) rounds.

Place into two 9-in. (23 cm) pie plates. Crimp the edges. Chill until ready for use.

Preheat oven to 350°F (180°C).

Filling : Blend together the almonds, sugar, egg whites and liqueur.

Spread the raspberry preserves on the bottom of each shell. Spoon the almond filling on top. Foil wrap the edges.

Bake in oven 55 to 60 minutes, or until nicely browned. Chill before serving.

Peach Meringue Shell

6 servings

4 cups	(1 L) sliced fresh peaches
2½ cups	(625 mL) fine sugar
6	egg whites
½ tsp	(3 mL) cream of tartar
1 tsp	(5 mL) white vanilla
1 tsp	(5 mL) cornstarch

Preheat oven to 225°F (105°C).

Sprinkle peaches with ½ cup (125 mL) of sugar. Set aside.

Whip the egg whites with the cream of tartar until very stiff.

Gradually beat in the remaining sugar.

Add the vanilla. Spoon meringue into 9-in. (23 cm) pie plate (making sure to push it up the sides).

Bake the pie shell in oven 15 to 20 minutes. Allow to cool and harden.

Drain the liquid from the peaches.

Pour peaches into meringue shell. Whip the cornstarch into peach liquid.

Heat in a small saucepan to thicken.

Pour over peaches and serve.

Blueberry Cheese Pie

8 servings

6 oz	(170 g) cream cheese
2	eggs
2 tbsp	(30 mL) heavy cream
1 tsp	(5 mL) grated lemon rind
4 cups	(1 L) blueberries, fresh or frozen
1	pie crust (see *Old-Fashioned Apple Pie*)
1 tbsp	(15 mL) lemon juice
¼ cup	(60 mL) apple juice
1 cup	(250 mL) sugar
2 tbsp	(30 mL) cornstarch

Preheat oven to 350°F (180°C).

Soften the cream cheese. Beat the eggs. Beat the cream cheese.

Add the cream to the eggs.

Fold in lemon rind and 2 cups (500 mL) of blueberries. Pour into pie shell.

Bake in oven 30 minutes. Remove.

In a saucepan, add the 2 cups (500 mL) of blueberries, lemon juice, apple juice, sugar and cornstarch. Blend thoroughly.

Heat over low heat until mixture thickens.

Pour on top of pie. Chill 3 hours.

Old-Fashioned Apple Pie

8 servings

Crust

¼ cup	*(60 mL)*	water
1		egg
1 tsp	*(5 mL)*	vinegar
2 cups	*(500 mL)*	flour
¼ cup	*(60 mL)*	cold butter
¼ cup	*(60 mL)*	cold shortening (lard)
½ tsp	*(3 mL)*	salt

Filling

5		apples, pared, cored and sliced
½ cup	*(125 mL)*	sugar
¼ tsp	*(1 mL)*	allspice
¼ tsp	*(1 mL)*	cinnamon
1 tbsp	*(15 mL)*	butter

Preheat oven to 400°F *(200°C)*.

Blend the water, egg and vinegar together. Place the flour in a mixing bowl. Cut in the butter and shortening. Add the salt. Blend in the liquid. Mix to a coarse meal texture. Divide into two. Place dough on a lightly floured surface. Roll into 12-in. *(30 cm)* rounds. Place one round into a 9-in. *(23 cm)* pie plate.

Mix together apples, sugar and spices. Spoon into pie shell. Dot with butter. Place second dough round over filling. Tuck top edge of pastry under bottom edge. Crimp to seal. Make several slits with small knife in upper crust. Bake in oven 40 minutes, or until pastry is golden brown.

Banana Cream Pie

2 pies

2		pie crusts (see *Old-Fashioned Apple Pie*)
3 cups	*(750 mL)*	milk
⅔ cup	*(160 mL)*	sugar
3		egg yolks
1 tbsp	*(15 mL)*	flour
1 tbsp	*(15 mL)*	butter
1 tbsp	*(15 mL)*	cornstarch
6 cups	*(1,5 L)*	sliced bananas
2 tsp	*(10 mL)*	banana extract

1 cup	*(250 mL)*	whipping cream

Preheat oven to 400°F *(200°C)*.

Line two 9-in. *(23 cm)* pie plates with pie crusts. Prick bottom and sides with fork.

Bake in oven 8 to 10 minutes.

Heat the milk and sugar together. Whip in the egg yolks.

Blend in the flour, butter and cornstarch. Add to milk and heat slowly until thickened.

Add the bananas and extract. Pour mixture into pie shells. Chill.

Whip the cream and pipe rosettes on the pies.

Banana Cream Pie

Brownies

Brownies

36 squares

¾ lb	(*340 g*) semi-sweet chocolate
¼ cup	(*60 mL*) honey
½ cup	(*125 mL*) butter
1 cup	(*250 mL*) sugar
2	eggs
1 tsp	(*5 mL*) vanilla
½ cup + 1 tbsp	(*140 mL*) flour
¼ tsp	(*1 mL*) baking powder
pinch	salt
3 tbsp	(*45 mL*) heavy cream
¼ cup	(*60 mL*) walnut pieces

Preheat oven to 350°F (*180°C*).

In a double boiler, melt half the chocolate and stir in the honey.

Cream together half the butter with ¼ cup (*60 mL*) of sugar until light and fluffy. Add the eggs one at a time. Add ½ tsp (*3 mL*) of vanilla. Stir in the melted chocolate.

Sift together the flour, baking powder and salt. Add to the creamed mixture.

Pour into a lightly buttered 9-in. (*23 cm*) square cake pan.

Bake in oven 20 to 25 minutes. Cool.

In a saucepan, blend the remaining sugar and butter with the cream. Bring to a boil.

Add the remaining chocolate, walnuts and vanilla. Stir until chocolate melts.

Pour over brownies. Cut into squares.

Poured Chocolate Icing

2½ cups (625 mL)

½ cup	(*125 mL*) light corn syrup
6 tbsp	(*90 mL*) water
5 tbsp	(*75 mL*) butter
1	300 g pkg. chocolate chips

Combine the corn syrup, water and butter in saucepan.

Bring to a rapid boil, stirring until butter is melted.

Remove from heat, add chocolate chips and cool to room temperature.

Pour over cake.

New York-Style Cheesecake

12-14 servings

Crust

3½ cups	(875 mL) graham cracker crumbs
1 tbsp	(15 mL) cinnamon
¼ cup	(60 mL) melted butter

Filling

5	250 g pkg. cream cheese, at room temperature
2 cups	(500 mL) sugar
1½ cups	(375 mL) heavy cream
2 tbsp	(30 mL) lemon juice
1 tbsp	(15 mL) vanilla
4	eggs, at room temperature
1½ cups	(375 mL) sour cream

Crust : Combine crust ingredients. Press into bottom and sides of 10-in. (25 cm) springform pan. Chill.
Preheat oven to 325°F (160°C).

Filling : Beat cream cheese and sugar until smooth. Add cream, lemon juice and vanilla; beat until well blended. Add the eggs, one at a time, beating well after each addition. Stir in sour cream.

Pour mixture into prepared shell and bake in oven until center is just set, about 90 minutes. Turn off oven and prop door open slightly.

After about 30 minutes, transfer to a rack to cool. Chill overnight. Serve with fresh fruit or a fruit sauce.

1

Combine crust ingredients and press into bottom and sides of a springform pan.

2

To make filling, beat cream cheese and sugar until smooth. Add cream, lemon juice and vanilla; blend well.

3

Add the eggs, one at a time, beating well after each addition.

4

Pour mixture into prepared shell and bake.

New York-Style Cheesecake

German Chocolate Turtle Cake

8-10 servings

Cake

¼ tsp	(*1 mL*) salt
1 tsp	(*5 mL*) baking soda
2½ cups	(*625 mL*) pastry flour
8 oz	(*225 g*) German chocolate
½ cup	(*125 mL*) boiling water
1 cup	(*250 mL*) butter
2 cups	(*500 mL*) sugar
4	egg yolks
1 tsp	(*5 mL*) vanilla
1 cup	(*250 mL*) heavy cream
4	egg whites

Preheat oven to 350°F (*180°C*).

Sift together the salt, baking soda and flour. Melt the chocolate in the boiling water.

Cream the butter and sugar until very light. Add the egg yolks one at a time.

Blend in the melted chocolate and vanilla. Add the flour and cream, ⅓ portions at a time.

Whip the egg whites until stiff. Fold gently into the batter.

Lightly butter three 8-in. (*20 cm*) round cake pans.

Bake in oven 35 to 40 minutes.

Cool 10 minutes before unmolding.

Filling

1¼ cups	(*310 mL*) brown sugar
½ cup	(*125 mL*) sugar
1⅓ cups	(*330 mL*) corn syrup
⅓ cup	(*80 mL*) butter
1 cup	(*250 mL*) condensed milk
½ tsp	(*3 mL*) vanilla
2 cups	(*500 mL*) walnut pieces

Combine the sugars and corn syrup together. Heat in a heavy saucepan.

Boil to 245°F (*118°C*) on a candy thermometer.

Add the butter, milk, vanilla and walnuts.

Return to 245°F (*118°C*).

Pour filling onto each cake layer top. Stack layers together.

Frosting

8 oz	(*225 g*) semi-sweet chocolate
½ cup	(*125 mL*) butter

In a double boiler, melt the chocolate.

Add the butter. Pour over cake and chill.

Serve cake once frosting is set.

Oatmeal Cookies

4 dozen

2 cups	(*500 mL*) flour
1 tsp	(*5 mL*) baking powder
1 tsp	(*5 mL*) baking soda
1 tsp	(*5 mL*) salt
1 cup	(*250 mL*) shortening
1 cup	(*250 mL*) brown sugar, firmly packed
1 cup	(*250 mL*) sugar
2	eggs
1 tsp	(*5 mL*) vanilla
2½ cups	(*625 mL*) quick-cooking oats

Preheat oven to 350°F (*180°C*).

Sift together the flour, baking powder, baking soda and salt. Set aside.

Cream together shortening and sugars until light and fluffy.

Add eggs one at a time, mixing well. Blend in vanilla.

Gradually add dry ingredients to creamed mixture. Stir in oats.

Shape into balls and place on a greased cookie sheet, 2 in. (*5 cm*) apart.

Bake 10 to 12 minutes.

Old-Fashioned Butter Drop Cookies

2 dozen

1¾ cups	(*430 mL*) flour
½ tsp	(*3 mL*) baking powder
½ tsp	(*3 mL*) baking soda
½ cup	(*125 mL*) butter
1 cup	(*250 mL*) sugar
1	egg
1 tsp	(*5 mL*) vanilla
¼ cup	(*60 mL*) milk

Preheat oven to 375°F (*190°C*).

Sift together the flour, baking powder and baking soda. Set side.

Cream together the butter and sugar until very light.

Add egg and blend well; mix in vanilla.

Gradually add dry mixture to creamed mixture. Slowly blend in milk.

Drop cookies on a greased cookie sheet, placing each 2 in. (*5 cm*) apart.

Bake 8 to 10 minutes.

Old-Fashioned Butter Drop Cookies

Ice Box Cookies

2 dozen

½ cup	(*125 mL*) butter
⅔ cup	(*160 mL*) sugar
1	egg
2 cups	(*500 mL*) flour
⅓ tsp	(*2 mL*) baking soda
½ tsp	(*3 mL*) cinnamon
½ tsp	(*3 mL*) nutmeg
pinch	salt

Preheat oven to 350°F (*180°C*).

Cream the butter with the sugar. Add the egg. Add the remaining ingredients.

Incorporate well and shape into a roll; wrap in wax paper.

Chill 4 to 6 hours or freeze. Unwrap and cut into 24 pieces.

Bake on a lightly buttered pastry sheet for 15 minutes.

Espagnole Sauce

6 cups (1,5 L)

4½ lbs	(*2 kg*) beef or veal bones
1	onion, diced
4	carrots, diced
3	celery stalks, diced
3	bay leaves
3	garlic cloves
2 tsp	(*10 mL*) salt
½ cup	(*125 mL*) flour
12 cups	(*3 L*) water
1	bouquet garni
1 cup	(*250 mL*) tomato purée
¾ cup	(*180 mL*) chopped leeks
3	parsley sprigs

Preheat oven to 450°F (*230°C*).

Put bones, onion, carrots, celery, bay leaves, garlic and salt in a roasting pan.

Bake 45 to 50 minutes until bones are nicely browned. Take care not to let them burn.

Sprinkle with flour and bake another 15 minutes.

Transfer ingredients to a stock pot. Swirl roasting pan with a little water. Pour drippings into stock pot.

Add all the remaining ingredients. Bring to a boil.

Reduce heat and simmer 3 to 4 hours or until half reduced.

Skim off all scum that rises to the top. Strain the sauce to remove bones, etc.

Then strain a second time through a cheesecloth.

Use as required.

Demi-Glace

1¾ cups (430 mL)

3 cups	(*750 mL*) Espagnole Sauce
1¼ cups	(*310 mL*) brown beef stock (see *Soups*)
¼ cup	(*60 mL*) sherry

Combine the Espagnole Sauce and beef stock.

Simmer until sauce is reduced in volume by two thirds.

Add sherry and use as required.

Mushroom and Parmesan Cream Sauce

2½ cups (625 mL)

1½ cups	(*375 mL*) sliced mushrooms
4 tsp	(*20 mL*) butter
4 tsp	(*20 mL*) all-purpose flour
¾ cup	(*180 mL*) chicken stock (see *Soups*)
¾ cup	(*180 mL*) heavy cream
2 tbsp	(*30 mL*) grated Parmesan cheese
	salt and pepper

Sauté the mushrooms in butter over high heat until tender.

Sprinkle with flour and cook, stirring, for 2 minutes.

Gradually stir in stock and cream; heat just to simmering.

Stir in Parmesan; season to taste.

Chicken Velouté

4 cups (1 L)

½ cup	(*125 mL*) butter
½ cup	(*125 mL*) flour
4 cups	(*1 L*) chicken stock (see *Soups*)

In a saucepan, melt the butter, add the flour and stir into a blond roux (paste).

Add the chicken stock and stir.

Simmer for 30 minutes.

Supreme Sauce

1 cup (250 mL)

1 cup	(*250 mL*) Chicken Velouté
1 cup	(*250 mL*) heavy cream
2 tbsp	(*30 mL*) cold butter

Over high heat, reduce chicken velouté to ½ cup (*125 mL*).

Whisk in the cream and continue reducing until the sauce is thickened and reduced to about 1 cup (*250 mL*).

Cut the butter into cubes and whisk in, a few cubes at a time, over medium heat.

Mornay Sauce

1¼ cups (310 mL)

2 tbsp	(30 mL)	butter
2 tbsp	(30 mL)	flour
½ cup	(125 mL)	chicken stock (see *Soups*)
½ cup	(125 mL)	heavy cream
¼ tsp	(1 mL)	salt
¼ tsp	(1 mL)	pepper
¼ cup	(60 mL)	grated Parmesan cheese

In a saucepan, melt the butter, add the flour and stir into a paste (roux).

Add the chicken stock, cream and seasonings.

Simmer, while stirring, until thickened.

Add cheese and simmer 2 more minutes.

Béchamel Sauce

1¼ cups (310 mL)

2 tbsp	(30 mL)	butter
2 tbsp	(30 mL)	flour
1 cup	(250 mL)	milk
¼ tsp	(1 mL)	salt
¼ tsp	(1 mL)	white pepper
pinch		nutmeg

Melt the butter in a saucepan. Add flour and stir into a paste (roux).

Add the milk and stir; simmer until thickened.

Add the seasonings and simmer 2 more minutes.

Béarnaise Sauce

¾ cup (180 mL)

3 tbsp	(45 mL)	white wine
1 tbsp	(15 mL)	dried tarragon leaves
½ tsp	(3 mL)	lemon juice
½ cup	(125 mL)	butter
3		egg yolks

Combine wine, tarragon and lemon juice in a small saucepan.

Over high heat, reduce to 2 tbsp (30 mL).

In another small saucepan, melt butter and heat almost to boiling.

In a blender or food processor, process egg yolks until blended.

With machine running, add butter in a slow, thin stream.

With machine off, add reduced wine mixture.

Process just until blended.

Honey-Mustard Sauce

1⅓ cups (330 mL)

⅔ cup	(160 mL)	mayonnaise (see *Dressings*)
⅓ cup	(80 mL)	honey
⅓ cup	(80 mL)	Dijon mustard

Blend all ingredients together. Chill.

White Wine Sauce

1¾ cups (430 mL)

3 tbsp	(45 mL)	butter
3 tbsp	(45 mL)	flour
½ cup	(125 mL)	chicken stock (see *Soups*)
½ cup	(125 mL)	heavy cream
½ cup	(125 mL)	white wine

In a saucepan, heat the butter. Add the flour. Cook for 2 minutes.

Add the liquids and simmer until thick.

Raspberry Coulis

3 cups (750 mL)

2¼ lbs	(1 kg)	raspberries
1 tbsp	(15 mL)	cornstarch
3 tbsp	(45 mL)	sherry
4 tbsp	(60 mL)	fine sugar

Purée raspberries in a food processor. Strain. Discard pulp and seeds.

Using 3 cups (750 mL) of raspberry juice, mix the cornstarch, sherry and sugar together.

Heat slowly until sauce thickens.

Use as required.

Index